Luis Jorge González

ENJOY YOUR INNER ARTIST

IMPROVING YOUR CREATIVITY WITH NLP

First Edition, December 14th, 1995.

Published for the copyright holder by

EDITORIAL FONT, S.A.
Padre Mier, 464 Ote.
Monterrey, N.L., MEXICO

Miembro de la Cámara Nacional
de la Industria Editorial Mexicana
Registro No. 1849

ISBN 968-7592-02-8

Front cover: CLAUDE MONET (1840-1926), *LES NYMPHÉAS/WATER-LILIES*.
            Oil on canvas (detail).

Printed and bound in Mexico.

DEDICATION

To the memory of my friend TODD EPSTEIN, who last year changed his way of living to the strains of the eternal music. I believe that he enjoys his inner artist as he plays heavenly melodies. In fact, he taught me—with examples taken from the world of music—that life is a symphony, full of harmony and beauty, in spite of pain and suffering. He taught me that NLP tiains us to know how to tune our spirit with the harmony of the whole creation. He taught me that being in tune we can play our part in that great symphony of life.

To John Grinder who, for the first time, opened before my eyes the horizon of NLP. To Judith DeLozier who taught me how to develop an artistic lifestyle. To Robert B.Dilts, my friend and constant teacher of NLP. To José I. Rodríguez A. with gratitude and admiration.

I appreciate the support of Fr. Camilo Maccise, my own Carmelite Community of Nairobi and Mexico, the participants in my workshops on "Psychology of Spirituality," and all the wonderful people I have met on the African continent.

CONTENTS

INTRODUCTION

I consider you, no matter who you are, like a great artist. Better, I would say that each of us is an artist. Sometimes, however, the artist in us is not born yet. He or she must be born and grow and flourish.

The purpose of this booklet is to help you to give birth to your inner artist, if this is the case. If you are already a painter, a pianist, a good professional, a committed housewife, a humourous storyteller, a proficient student, and so on, I acknowledge that your inner artist is born.

Still, it might be that your artistic capabilities need to grow. Your inner artist is capable of further development. You can become a more brilliant artist. Yet you may feel you do not have the ability to overcome certain obstacles. Let us say that sometimes you feel stuck or lacking the necessary inspiration to work more creatively. In such situations you will profit from the exercises you will find in this booklet.

As you have noticed, I am using the word *artist* in a wider sense. I presuppose you can be an artist without being devoted to any sort of art. Without being a painter, an architect, a musician, a poet or something like that, you can be an artist in the way you live, dress, or cut your hair, the manner in which you work or treat other people, and so forth.

I received the idea of living artistically during a workshop on NLP—*Neuro-Linguistic Programming*—at the University of California in Santa Cruz. It was John Grinder and Judith DeLozier who gave me this perspective in 1989. The possibility of having a creative life impregnated with beauty, harmony and sensibility sounded nice.

In fact, Grinder had displayed his creativity in a wonderful way. He launched, in the early '70s, together with Richard

Bandler, this new trend in science which we know as **NLP.** This and other discoveries they introduced, enriched the world with a new model that empowers people to become creative or even more creative.[1]

Judith DeLozier is one of the co-developers of NLP. She worked—in the company of Leslie Cameron-Bandler and Robert Dilts—with Grinder and Bandler in the initial development of NLP. Judy is a professional ballet dancer. Her Ph.D. is in Anthropology of Religion. Therefore, her movements, gestures, words and attitudes offer suggestions about *how* to live an artistic life.

I really do not know *why* Grinder and Judy DeLozier came to the conclusion that our lives can be artistic. Nevertheless, I thank them for such an idea.

Through them I discovered a new horizon of possibilities. Regardless of your field of professional activities, personal situation, status, sex and religious beliefs you can become a real artist.

NLP provides us with different ways, perspectives and tools that facilitate the process of becoming the artist each of us is meant to be. You have access to NLP through workshops, talks, books and interviews with NLP trainers.

---

[1] If you want to know more about NLP, consult the books by Grinder and Bandler, Robert B.Dilts, and other NLP authors that appear in the bibliography of this book. In brief, *Neuro* refers to our *neurological* resources that operate through our senses—seeing, hearing, feeling, smelling and tasting. The word *linguistic* points out the resources contained in words, language and thoughts. And *programming* suggests that each human being is a *programme*. And a programme means a plan to attain a goal by choosing the best alternatives. In fact, according to J.Z.Young, author of the books *Programs of the Brain,* we are programmed for self-conservation and, therefore, health and happiness are the best indicators as to whether we are attaining that central goal of life. In conclusion, NLP is the science that teaches how to use the neurological and linguistic resources in order to follow the program of self-preservation, health and happiness in union with other people and nature.

I will offer you some essential tools and exercises applied to creativity. I hope they will assist you in the pleasant adventure of awakening the artist that you really are.

I suggest you walk on a path of seven stages. Each one of these has seven steps. And you are expected to take one step a day. Simultaneously, you are supposed to accomplish certain tasks that are simple and do not demand too much time. Some of them are weekly assignments and others are daily requirements like eating or sleeping. All these activities have the specific goal of awakening your artist within.

You may wonder, perhaps, why we need to awaken or improve our inner artist. My answer will be one of my favourite ones. I really believe you and anyone is an artist. When the artist you are becomes fully alive and active, you become the person you are meant to be. You were created as a programme with a central goal: to become a person. But you require all your creativity to exploit the talents and resources you have been endowed with to attain that goal.

I really believe that creativity belongs to the core of your *identity*. You *are* creative. You *are* an artist. The Creator endowed life with a creative energy. But God created human beings in such a way that we *are* more creative than other living creatures. The reason is that He created man and woman in His likeness and in His own image. In consequence, you possess a creative being similar, in its own proportion, to God's being. So, you cannot *not* be creative. If you are a human creature you are a creator. You are an artist. You cannot escape from your very being.

In my own experience, creativity is unavoidable. You cannot avoid being an artist. Sometimes you employ your creativity to make somebody else angry or disappointed. Very often you use it to smile in a way that your face becomes a masterpiece. Some days your voice sounds so enthusiastic and convincing that even the best speaker would envy you.

Certainly, possessing a greater awareness of your creative capabilities is a distinct advantage. If you know them and use them, you will be like a good entrepreneur who knows the amount of his capital and, therefore, is able to invest his money in the best way.

Hopefully this booklet may empower you not only to know the rich amount of your talents, but also to use them. NLP aims to show the practical way for a person to know *how* to make use of his or her resources. And you can learn how to display your talents to live artistically.

The seven stages to follow to develop your inner artist contain different exercises. They are the fruit of my therapeutic experience. But they are also the result of a personal research on Jesus' creativity. Searching for the secrets of the Lord's creativity, I have discovered seven main creative traits. He felt the *need and responsibility of being creative.* Jesus experienced the *joy of dreaming* and the *power of producing new ideas.* He transformed his ideas into a *creative action.* Instead of being a victim of his *inner critic,* he used it to discern the best ideas and to achieve important discoveries. Finally, Jesus gave to his activity a double orientation, that is, towards a *social creativity* and a *spiritual creativity.*

In brief, during your creative journey you will go through the following seven stages:

1. NEED AND RESPONSIBILITY OF BEING CREATIVE
2. THE JOY OF DREAMING
3. NEW IDEAS THROUGH SYSTEMIC THINKING
4. THE CREATIVE ACTION
5. THE RESOURCES OF THE INNER CRITIC
6. SOCIAL CREATIVITY
7. SPIRITUAL CREATIVITY

Nairobi, Kenya, August 15, 1995.

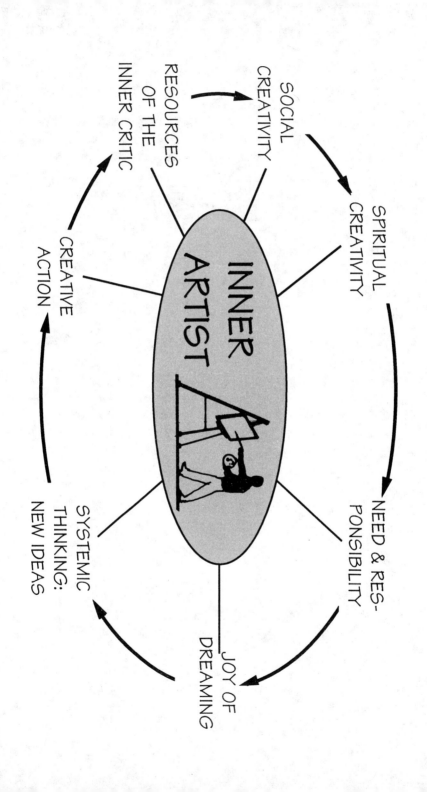

I- NEED & RESPONSIBILITY OF BEING CREATIVE

More than a *need,* creativity is a pleasure. And more than a *responsibility,* it is a joy. Nevertheless, I have chosen such a title for this chapter, because I believe that creativity comes from within. It is your inner artist who will yield the expressions of your creative talents.

In fact, you are the one who will experience, like a deep drive, the need to produce new ideas, to transform them into inventions and to verify—together with your inner critic—if you are getting the results you really want.

But there are moments when you will feel stuck, or lacking inspiration, or unwilling to take on your creative tasks. In such situations you will take action only with the inner push of your decision. By displaying your personal freedom, you will assume the responsibility of being creative. You will recognise the rich treasure of talents you have received from above and you will freely decide to make use of them.

In both cases, whether you experience the need of being creative or you choose to be so, you will certainly feel pleasant vibrations within your body. Creativity, by its very nature, represents an inexhaustible fountain of happiness.

The need of being creative does not originate in a selfish desire to satisfy ourselves. Of course, criminals, corrupt politicians, drug addicts and pushy people who will step on anyone's toes out of greed or ambition, experience the need of being creative. And they are very creative. But their creativity is not the one that humankind requires to have a better and more beautiful world. Still worse, their creativity is unable to give them the happiness they long for. On the contrary, their destructive creativity not only causes a lot of suffering in many people, but also makes them selfish, resentful, bitter, anxious, and deeply unhappy.

The kind of creativity that makes us happy, joyful and healthy, comes from the will to serve others. This kind of creativity empowers our inner artist to transform our world and society. It enables each of us to create the healthy, peaceful, just, loving and happy world we all want to belong to.

What's more, if you put forth this sort of creativity, you will get not only pleasure and peace, but also money. There are witnesses to this fact in our society. For instance, Yoshiro NakaMats. He is the most prolific inventor in human history. Before him, it was Thomas Alva Edison with 1,093 patents. Whereas NakaMats holds more than 2,300. He has invented the floppy disk and licensed the technology to IBM. And he gets a royalty on the millions of disks sold every year all over the world. Among his inventions are the compact disc, the compact disc player, the digital watch, etc. Well, this man says:

> "My rationale is very simple: we *need* to open up the world. We *need* to share and to interact. I always tell young inventors to forget about money as a primary motivator and to concentrate on ideas that will benefit mankind. If you do this, the money will automatically follow! And, by inventions, I don't just mean visible items. There are invisible inventions too."[1]

A.Robbins, who has popularised NLP and has earned lots of money, has a similar suggestion. He writes:

> *"The key to wealth is to be more valuable.* If you have more skills, more ability, more intelligence, specialised knowledge, a capacity to do things few others can do, or if you just think creatively and contribute on a massive scale, you can earn more than

---

[1] Quoted by C.C.Thompson, *What a Great Idea!* New York, NY: HarperCollins, 1992, p. xv.

you ever thought possible. The single most important and potent way to expand your income is to *devise a way to consistently add real value to people's lives, and you will prosper...* The true purpose of any corporation is to create products and services that increase the quality of life for all the customers they serve. If this is achieved on a consistent basis, then profit is absolutely assured."[2]

The product or service you can invent might be *invisible*. Think of a new way of teaching, a new way to spark creativity in others, a way to overcome negative feelings. These invisible inventions, of course, increase the quality of life for all people. And your reward will be emotional, social, financial, and even spiritual.

1. THE GOAL OF CREATIVITY: PEOPLE

From the most practical perspective, people represent the central goal of creativity. Even when your invention is a piece of art or a mathematical formula, you are adding real value to people's lives. Sooner or later you will reap the fruits of such creativity. At least your descendants will collect those fruits.

In any case, one of the most basic steps to awaken the artist within is the creation of new and richer relationships. You can meet more people. Even more, you can meet them in a new way and at a deeper level. If you try this, you will allow your inner artist to take action.

1) *Meet new people in a new and deeper way.* This first exercise aims at people. Its intention is to transform them into a

[2] A.Robbins, *Awaken the Giant within.* New York, NY: Simon & Schuster, 1991, pp. 476-478.

trigger of your creative resources. You will use your *focus* and your *sensory acuity* with more awareness and more fun.

1- Think of those people you would like to meet, of those you will probably meet, and of those you would never expect to meet.

2- Let your inner artist feel completely free. Encourage him to represent the most incredible people as well as the strangest, most disgusting ones. Let him focus on their peculiarities.

3- Use your senses to capture the most peculiar traits, behaviours and attitudes of one representative of each group (those you would like to meet, those you will probably meet, and those you do not expect to meet). See them, listen to them, feel and smell them.

4- Imagine, as vividly as possible, a specific encounter with each of those three people.

5- In order to establish a relationship that a) is new or different from your habitual relations, and   b) happens on a deeper level:

> A- How is your first greeting for each of them?
> B- How are: a) your voice tone, b) the way you look at them, c) your facial expressions, d) your body posture?
> C- Which questions do you ask in order to achieve your goal (new and deeper relations)?
> D- What do you tell them, as you try to get closer to your goal?
> E- How do you know you are achieving your goal?
> F- What do you do if what you are doing does not get you closer to your goal?
> G- How do you feel as you imagine yourself reaching your goal?

6- Using the above steps, plan a new and deeper encounter with a specific person. It can be a relative, a friend, a colleague, a neighbour, etc.

7- Take action. Let your inner artist enjoy the process of having a new and deeper relationship.

8- Repeat the exercise with as many people as possible. Transform this exercise into a habit in your daily life.

This exercise represents the first step of your creative journey. As I have already suggested, you are supposed to take one step each day. But, simultaneously, you have another activity for today.

From today on, you will give your inner artist the opportunity to express her- or himself. It is much better if you get up ten minutes earlier each morning. Take a notebook or a sheet of paper, and write down whatever comes to your mind.

The goal now is *freedom*. Allow yourself to write what you have never expressed to anyone: your weirdest, craziest, most negative ideas. The purpose is to unleash your inner artist. So, it may happen that he/she complains or blames, or confesses creative and productive impotence.

Write at least one page a day. Better if you write two or three. In the morning your mind—your inner artist—may be freer, more spontaneous. That is why getting up ten minutes earlier is important. Try your best. If not, find a specific moment when you can assign yourself ten minutes to unleash your mind.

Certainly, you must keep your daily pages in secret. Knowing that nobody is going to read them makes it easier for you to be spontaneous and free while you are writing. Even you, at least for one year, should avoid reading what you have written.

Finally, according to my own experience, your daily pages are more important than many other creative exercises. Do not skip them. Better to omit one of the exercises here suggested than to skip your daily pages.[3]

Today's last exercise is very simple. Just ask yourself, as many times as possible, "What's the most beautiful thing here and now? When you have the answer, just enjoy that beauty for a while.

2. PEOPLE'S NEEDS

On this second day I presuppose that you are creating new and deeper relationships with people. I am concerned with the type of innovation and depth you are getting in your human relations. It is enough that you are able to produce a change or a difference to your habitual way of relating with others.

If you have taken that step, you are ready for the second one. But before I describe today's step, let me suggest that you ask yourself, "What's most beautiful here and now?"

I am, incidentally, taking for granted that you have already written your daily pages.

Then, while you enjoy the beauty that is present before you, try to intensify the pleasure of knowing more about people's needs. What they require and long for might be a kind of request that awakens your inner artist.

1- As you delight in something nice, take a piece of paper and jot down all the different needs that specific people have at present. Call to mind all kinds of people from all over the world.

---

[3] I learnt this technique of the "morning pages" from J.Cameron with M.Bryan, *The Artist's Way*. New York, NY: G.P.Putnam's Sons, 1992. I write my daily pages every day. They help me a lot.

2- Make a long, long list of human needs. What matters now is quantity not quality. If possible, work together with others. Have at least a group of two.

   3- Classify those needs. Sort out:
   A- The most urgent needs
   B- The most important in the long term
   C- The final ones[4]

4- Choose one of these three groups. Focus on the individual needs. Pay attention to their most specific features. Employ the visual *submodalities:* make them closer, brighter, colourful, bigger, clearer... Emphasise the oral expression of those needs with the auditory submodalities, i.e. their voice is clear, loud, close, low, slow...

5- Ask yourself, "What can I do for them?" Do not search for a solution; what's more, gently avoid solutions for the time being. But insist on asking yourself, "What can I do for them?"

6- Allow your unconscious mind to work by itself. As you know, your unconscious mind carries out the essential programme of your life which is self-preservation together with health and happiness. Your unconscious mind takes care of many activities you pay no attention to: breathing, digesting, growing new cells, repairing damaged ones, purifying toxins, preserving hormonal balance, converting stored energy from fat to blood sugar, raising and lowering blood pressure, maintaining steady body temperature, etc. So, your unconscious mind can help—during this period of incubation—to find out your possible contribution to satisfy those needs.

---

[4] These correspond somehow to the "metaneeds" which Maslow discovered in self-actualising people. Cf. A.H.Maslow, *Motivation and Personality.* New York, NY: Harper & Row, 1970, pp. 149-180. If you ask yourself, "Why do I want money?" you will probably answer, "With money I can buy food." "Why do want food?" "To live."

7- Take a deep breath, relax, and bask in what is most beautiful for you just now.

For the rest of today keep your focus on people's needs. Open your senses, as much as possible, to notice the needs of people living around you.

Keep your senses open as well to beauty. Perceive the beautiful line of a car, the harmony of music, the taste of an orange, the smell of your wife's perfume, the touch of your daughter who kisses you, and so on.

3. PEOPLE'S POSSIBILITIES

On this third day, you and your group will continue the research or exploration that you started yesterday. But this time you will pay more attention to the highest needs of people, or metaneeds. Usually, the word *possibility* presupposes that you have satisfied your basic needs. That, for instance, you are properly able to accomplish your tasks as a student, secretary, housewife, physician, businessman, politician, artist, etc. In consequence, you have satisfied your labour needs. However, you may go beyond your present standard. You might raise your expectations and goals. In this case, you will inquire what your possibilities are; in which aspects you could improve your present performance.

I know that Yoshiro NakaMats and other inventors adopt this perspective. They are in search of further possibilities. Artists, geniuses, saints, great leaders, and so on, proceed from the same perspective. As they look for other possibilities, they make important discoveries. As a result, they enrich our world with innovations and inventions.

Now it is time to search for possibilities. Besides writing your daily pages and enjoying the beauty around you, do the following exercise.

1- Be sure that your emotional state is joyful. Help yourselves by focusing on something beautiful. Take two or three minutes to really derive pleasure from that beauty. Open your senses and associate yourselves with the qualities that render the focused object beautiful.

2- Recall the people you have been thinking of in the last two days. Call to your mind not only people who are poor and needy, but even great, holy, and successful people.

3- Explore now how they can develop themselves, to improve, to be excellent... Remember Pascal's dictum, "Man surpasses man infinitely."

4- Make a long list of all the possibilities you can envisage. Quantity not quality is what matters now.

5- Classify those possibilities. Sort out:
   A- The most important
   B- The most beneficial
   C- The most viable

6- Give your inner artist the opportunity to work by her- or himself. He/she is deeply associated with your unconscious mind. I would not know how to distinguish one from the other. Therefore, ask yourselves, "What other possibilities are fluttering around them?" And let your inner artist explore and discover further possibilities, especially as you sleep tonight.

7- To close the exercise take two or three deep breaths. Feel the air that comes in and out of your chest. Add the pleasure of breathing deeply to the joy of searching for further possibilities. This kind of research involves, normally, very pleasant feelings.

4. FEELING PEOPLE'S NEEDS AND POSSIBILITIES

This time, you will try to experience people's needs and possibilities in your heart or even in your gut. Usually we watch people's suffering—Rwanda, Bosnia, Cuba, etc.—at a distance. In NLP terms, we are *dissociated,* i.e. we put an invisible barrier of numbness between them and ourselves. We become like cold observers who do not involve their feelings at all.

I find this attitude correct from the clinical point of view. If we *associate* ourselves with all kinds of people's problems and opportunities, we risk going crazy. Our sensibility cannot take so much.

In certain situations, however, and having an empowering reason to do so, we should open our senses completely. For instance, you may involve your heart and feelings in people's needs and opportunities in order to awaken the creator within. Need is the spur of creativity for many people. Street children deploy their inventiveness under the spur of hunger.

Once people's needs and possibilities have resounded in your heart, from my own experience I suggest you move into another perceptual position.

In NLP we distinguish, at least, three different perspectives to face people and the world:

1st position	=	ACTOR (you are yourselves and *associated).*
2nd position	=	PARTNER *(dissociated,* you put yourselves in other people's skin and mind).
3rd position	=	OBSERVER *(dissociated,* you just watch people from a distance).

In *1st position* you open the doors of your soul, that are your senses, and allow people and their emotions—sadness, anger, anxiety, peace, love and joy—to flood your heart. In *2nd position* you open your senses but from other people's or a partner's perception of their own reality. You do not get involved in their feelings. You just understand their point of view, that is, their own maps of the world, their situation, their experience. In *3rd position* you observe both yourself and your partner. You are aware of the interaction between the two. You become a kind of film director. Therefore, you are in the best position to use your creativity.

An artist is able to shift from one position to another in order to achieve beautiful creations. So, I think it is important you enjoy life looking at people and circumstances from 1st, 2nd and 3rd positions.

Later on I will explain other positions which, like the 3rd, are very appropriate for displaying your creative talents. In the following exercise I will encourage you to use those three: 1st, 2nd and 3rd.

1- Breathe deeply three times. Be conscious of what is beautiful around you at present. Pay attention to the beauty you are watching or listening to. Allow feelings of gladness to grow and to vibrate in your bodies.

2- Choose a human need and approach it, either individually or in a group, from different perspectives.

3- Each of you is invited to face that need from *1st position*. Open your senses and your heart. Feel that need with your body and soul. Remember a time when you had a similar need. Using the stimulus of your own memories, experience people's suffering. "Weep with them that weep" (Rom 12:15).

4- After some minutes, shake off that state of sorrow and pain. Immediately change your perceptual position. In a rather detached state, go inside people's hearts and minds. Try to see things as they do. Try to use their own maps of reality. Try to understand the feelings they create through their own interpretations of reality. In this *2nd position* you cannot feel any pain, since you are not in your own body, so to speak, but in other people's positions.

5- Once you have tried *1st* and *2nd* positions, you are ready to experience the *3rd* one. Imagine yourselves in a corner of the room or floating on the air in such a way that you can observe from there both yourselves and people. As if you were watching a movie, explore the possible interaction between you and people in need.

6- Still from *3rd position,* find out the possibilities people have to satisfy that specific need. Maybe you can give them a hand, so that their possibilities may become a reality.

7- Keeping your *3rd position,* think of further possibilities those people have. After you have found some, relate them in some way with yourselves.

8- From your *3rd position* come back to *1st.* Breathe deeply, feel your feet touching the ground and enjoy being able to see and hear. Be aware of the nicest aspect of your environment. Stretch yourselves and be ready to have fun as you change your perceptual positions during the rest of this day.

5. THE NEED OF SOLUTIONS

As soon as you feel the need of solutions or the drive to find them, your inner artist is operating. If you relate the artist with your unconscious mind, it is much easier to understand that each of you, by your own nature, is a creator. Think of your unconscious mind that every day replaces from 300 to 800 billion dead cells in your body, and you will be convinced of your creative identity.

Your daily pages are intended to free your inner artist. He is very creative, but human cultures prevent him from displaying his resources and abilities. Each day's exercises are designed to achieve the same purpose.

In today's exercise you are not supposed to come out with solutions. It is enough that you feel the need to create them. But if you get good ideas, jot them down. Later on you will make use of them.

1- Relax. This time ask yourselves, "What's the best of the best I or we have now?" Search not for what is nice, but for whatever is good or beneficial in your life. As you become aware of the best thing, quality or person you have, derive pleasure from such a gift.

2- Represent in your mind, now, a specific need you have discovered in people. Make a drawing of it on a sheet of paper. The aesthetics do not matter in this case. Draw that need just as you want.

3- Take another piece of paper, perhaps a bigger one. Make the image or symbol for that need bigger, use colours, make it alive, suggest a kind of movement in it, and give it clarity and attractiveness.

4- Now imagine background music for that picture. Add people's voices. Write down their words and specify the volume, tone, tempo, pauses and location of their voices.

5- Go into *1st position* and try to feel, as much as possible, a deep and urgent need of finding out solutions. Make that need stronger until you sense it in your own body.

6- Share with another person or with your group the process you have followed to make your need of solutions stronger. At least describe to them the experience of your creative drive here and now.

7- Next, make a long list of reasons to feel pleasure if you discover or invent solutions. But invoke reasons that you believe in or that you can feel in your gut. Share this list with somebody else if you are doing the exercise by yourself.

8- Answer the question, "Why is it important to create solutions?" Collect as many answers as possible. Write them down on a piece of paper. Share your personal discoveries with your group or with your friends.

9- Close the exercise with a sort of mental movie in which you appear creating solutions, sharing them with people, and applying them in a group. Imagine a picture you might use to draw the results. Share your movie and picture with others. Try to produce a common picture or even a movie. What would it be like?

10- Breathe deeply. Put a big grin on your faces. Enjoy each other's smiles.

6. THE POWER OF LOVE

I believe that love is one of the strongest reasons we may have to allow our inner artist to act. When you really love someone, you *create* her or him. You create them in the sense of giving yourself as a source of the necessary conditions for their growth. Your own congruence, understanding (2nd position), unconditional acceptance and warmth create an atmosphere where others can be, and grow, and reach their fullness. Without such conditions they cannot be the persons they are meant to be.

I totally agree with Dr. Victor Frankl who writes:

"Love is the only way to grasp another human being in the innermost core of his personality. No one can become fully aware of the very essence of another human being unless he loves him. By his love he is enabled to see the essential traits and features in the beloved person; and even more, he sees that which is potential in him, which is not yet actualized but yet ought to be actualized. Furthermore, by his love, the loving person enables the beloved person to actualize these potentialities. By making him aware of what he can be and what he should become, he makes these potentialities come true."[5]

So, love has the power to achieve the highest creation we might ever imagine. Not only that, love starts the process of creating a human being. Love drives a couple towards sexual intercourse which, sooner or later, will be the origin of a new human creature.

On the other hand, love must complete the masterpiece wrought by the couple. The new human being must become a person. And this transformation takes place as a result of love. Beyond the sexual or marital love, a deeper love like parental love, therapeutic love, or friendly love is required to facilitate the process of becoming a person.

Unconditional love, therefore, is able to create the beloved person. He or she becomes a real person—*unique, self-aware, responsible, free* and *able to love*—when he/she has the experience of unconditional love.

Today we are going to awaken the inner artist through the experience of unconditional love. Our inner artist, I believe, is the deepest source of our potential to love other people and ourselves. So, whenever we put ourselves in a state of love, our inner artist is active and happy.

1- Breathe deeply three times. Wonder what is nice and good in your present environment. Focus on the nicest and best things here and now. Delight in those two things or persons or aspects of reality.

2- Remember an experience of giving or receiving unconditional love. See what you were seeing at that moment. Listen to what you were probably hearing. Feel in your body the pleasant sensations you felt then. Repeat the same process with two or three other similar experiences.

[5] V.E.Frankl, *Man's Search for Meaning*. New York, NY: Pocket, 1985, p. 134.

3- As you feel a state of overflowing love, plan in your mind to express it to somebody who is friendly and loving with you. Allow her/his love to stir up your present state of love.

4- Now recall the picture you have made of one specific person's need. Does your state of love increase your need or will to create solutions? If not, what is the difference? How does love affect your previous urge to create solutions? Is love a good state to be creative?

5- Make a picture of your future. See yourselves living more and more frequently in a state of love. Observe your reactions, attitudes and actions in the face of people's needs and possibilities. Imagine feeling the loving impulse to enhance the quality of life in other people.

6- Breathe deeply several times. As you breathe deeply, experience the increase of energy in your bodies. Be ready to really express your love to other people.

7. INSTRUMENTS OF THE ETERNAL CREATOR

I agree with those who believe that human creativity is a share in God's own creative power. Julia Cameron suggests, for instance, that "creativity is God's gift to us." And she adds, "When we open ourselves to exploring our creativity, we open ourselves to God." "Our creative dreams and yearnings come from a divine source. As we move toward our dreams, we move toward our divinity."[6]

From the NLP perspective, Robert Dilts interviewed the inventor Lowell Noble and asked what was the best perspective to eventually achieve an invention. Lowell answered:

"I think that there are basically three perspectives that people visualize things from: 1) what I would call the God's eye

---

[6] J.Cameron with M.Bryan, *The Artist's Way*, o.c., p. 3.

view; it's like looking down at the earth, a long ways away; 2) then there is the driver view, where you are seeing what you would be seeing if you were actually there, like actually driving a car, or actually sitting in front of the optics bench; 3) then there is the right-shoulder view, where you've visualized yourself from a short distance away, usually slightly up and behind. Those are three basic ways of visualizing systems. In visualizing a whole system, the God's eye view is the best, then the driver view, and then the right-shoulder view."[7]

When I recognise human creativity as a gift of God I do not forget that He has given us the gift of freedom and autonomy as well. We are free to find out the best perspective to enhance our creativity and achieve our inventions. In fact, Lowell Noble recommends the "God's eye view" as the best.

Robert Fritz, with a long experience in creativity, emphasises the effective power of human creativity. It is a real gift. God has given it to each of us once, and forever. That is why Fritz clarifies:

> "To talk about transcendence by saying, 'I am nothing but a channel' or 'I am nothing but a tool of God's will,' is a misunderstanding of the relationship between you and that special moment focused through you as creator. The notion that human action is inessential in the creative process distorts the power, beauty, and unique preciousness of the individuality of the human spirit."[8]

In brief, as images of God, human creatures share in God's unlimited and eternal creative power. We are creative by nature. Our creativity is God's gift to us. We please Him when we are creative. The child who is sent by his father to the best school and

---

[7] R.B.Dilts, T.Epstein, R.W.Dilts, *Tools for Dreamers.* Cupertino, CA, Meta Publications, 1991, p. 173.

[8] R.Fritz, *The Path of Least Resistance.* New York, NY: Fawcett Columbine, 1989, p. 279.

makes the most of his opportunity and talents, prolongs his father's own creativity. In that sense, he becomes an instrument of his father's creativity.

After these clarifications, let us move to step seven of our creative journey. Today we are going to get in touch, through faith and love, with our eternal Creator.

1- Take a comfortable body posture. Breathe deeply and slowly several times. Fix your eyes on something nice without blinking. When your eyes get tired shut them gently.

2- Acknowledge the presence of God—as you believe He is—within yourselves. Through Jesus, He has said: "Anyone who loves me will keep my word, and my Father will love him, and we shall come to him and make a home in him" (Jn 14:23).

3- In the light of your faith, use your imagination to represent God's loving eyes and, if you are a Christian, look at Jesus' cheerful countenance. Realise their infinite and eternal love for you.

4- Acknowledge that because of His unlimited love, the eternal Creator has enriched you with the gift of creativity.

5- Visualise or describe your own innermost core as the most beautiful and pleasant place you have ever seen or imagined. Your personal centre is so beautiful because it has been created in God's likeness and God dwells therein.

6- Imagine yourselves sitting before the Lord. Enjoy His beauty which is the source of any created beauty we can see in the universe. Compare all the beauty of the universe with God's beauty and realise that God's beauty is infinitely superior.

7- Now adore the Lord God, paying *loving attention* to Him. You may repeat a sentence of love like, "Lord, I love You." "Lord, I love You." "Lord, I love You."

8- After 10 minutes in an attitude of adoration tell the Lord that, from today on, you have decided to lead a creative life. Out of love for Him and other people, decide to be an artist in all you think, feel and do.

9- Ask for God's grace and help in order to persevere. Facing big problems or negative people you will require God's grace to be creative in spite of them.

10- Prepare to open your eyes. Before you do, breathe deeply several times. Feel the energy and vigour you are getting through your breathing. Enjoy the source of peace, joy, love, beauty and creativity you have within yourselves, that is, God the eternal Creator. Slowly, move your fingers, hands, arms, shoulders, neck, head, feet, legs... As if you were stretching yourselves after a pleasant sleep, be ready to open your eyes. Now, open your eyes.

After this short encounter with the eternal Creator, if you want, make a contract with Him. Commit yourselves to have a creative and artistic life from today on. Your commitment is more effective if you write it down.

Of course, you can use your own creativity by inventing the text of your commitment. Nevertheless, I offer you a suggestion just to enhance your creativity. If you prefer, you may establish this contract with a person, with your own group, with yourselves.

Contract

"Lord, I, _____, believe I am an artist. You have created me in your own image; that is why I am creative by nature. Therefore, I commit myself to the seven-week duration of this creative journey. I, _____, undertake to write my daily pages, to practise a daily exercise, to enjoy the best and most beautiful feelings at each moment.

I, _____, really want to think and act creatively in order to please you and improve the quality of

---

life in other people. At home, at work, driving, exercising, talking to others, praying and so on, I will exert my creativity.

I, _____, foresee some emotional reactions during this creative journey, and I am ready to deal with them in a positive and creative way. Because of that, I, _____, commit myself to excellent self-care—adequate sleep, healthy nutrition, exercise, and some minutes of silent prayer (meditation)—for the duration of this journey. I rely on your grace and love.

_____
(signature)

_____
(date)

Intentions

The power of *intentions* has been rediscovered in medical research. People suffering from a certain kind of Parkinson's disease who are unable to walk, take a step forward when they hear a stimulating sentence. Though technically impossible from a neurological point of view, intent can trigger near miraculous motions.

It is important here to say the words *I want* with all the strength of our body, heart and mind. On the other hand, I believe, like Dr. Chopra, that our intention is more effective when we connect it with God's power. That is why I place first an invocation of the Lord.

Of course, you are going to invent your own intentions. But for the moment, you may use the following:

— Lord, I *want* to be creative to please you.
— Lord, in your likeness, I *want* to be a real artist.
— Lord, I *want* to be creative on behalf of people.
— Lord, I *want* to rejoice in the beauty of this world.
— Lord, I *want* to be a creator of beauty in all my thoughts, feelings and deeds.
— Lord, I *want* to compliment the beauty of people's attitudes and works.
— Lord, I *want* to invent things or processes that add value to people's lives.
— Lord, I *want* to accomplish works that make this world more beautiful and enjoyable for people.
— Lord, I *want* to see, hear and feel people's needs to imagine solutions and structural changes in our society.
— Lord, I *want* to live a constant state of love to improve my creativity.
— Lord, I *want* to be the constant creator of my life in union with you and people.
— Lord, I *want* to express the originality and uniqueness of my identity.

II- THE JOY OF DREAMING

The first step of any human creation is dreaming. In our dreams we often represent our desires, what we do not have yet, but yet ought to be transformed into a reality.

A painter first dreams, then gets some ideas, plans the execution of his picture, and finally takes action.

The same process is followed for any human accomplishment. Artists, workers, housewives, students, teachers, physicians, psychotherapists, social workers, politicians, religious leaders have their own dreams first. A woman dreams of having a child. A doctor dreams of getting his patients cured. A musician dreams the melody he would like to compose. And so forth.

Dreaming is basic in human development. Without dreams human history would not exist. Progress in any human area is a result of people's dreams.

The first step to change, improve and transform the world and ourselves is dreaming. Once you have a dream, the forces of nature, life and humankind are awakened. Sooner or later that dream will become a reality.

Of course, as you can imagine, I am talking about dreams that, in one way or another, benefit our world and humankind.

On the other hand, I make a distinction between *dreams* and *ideas*. Ideas may be more specific, practical and context-related. Dreams, on the other hand, might be more distant, abstract and global.

Certainly, sometimes dreams are specific and viable, while our ideas refer to a very distant goal. That is true. But, for practical reasons, I will assume that *ideas* describe short-term goals that are specific, realistic, affordable and useful. Whereas I will take for granted that *dreams* turn out to be long-term goals. Thus, they are distant, global, visionary.

1. DRIVEN BY HOPE

The force that drives us towards our dreams is hope. the engine that moves people towards their dreams is hope. This attitude of hope yields an emotional state of trust and certainty that makes people prone to use their resources to reach the desired goal.

In NLP we say that our *resources* make up the bridge which takes us from *present state* to *desired state*. However, the personal or group state of hope conjures up not only a utopia or a dream, but also the will to take action. Hope offers the strength we need to use our resources and walk toward our dreams.

If a cancerous person does not have hope, he or she will give up. In consequence, they will prevent their immune system from taking action. And without the healthy resources of the immune system, the abnormal cells of cancer will spread.

So, *hope* has a specific place in any process of change and, especially, to materialise the big dreams of humankind, different nations and religious institutions. Together with our resources we need hope. Let us visualise the role of hope in the NLP scheme for change.

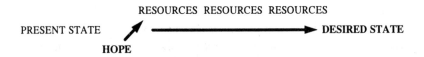

The practice of *hope* requires at least four main elements:

1) Visualising a better future, 2) trusting in something or someone, 3) visualizing enjoyment of a good future, 4) readiness to take action.

A- *Visualisation*

You probably wonder what is meant by the verb "visualise." Normally, it means to see internally, i.e. in your mind, a sort of picture, or photograph, or a movie. But some people do the equivalent by listening to a voice that narrates what is present in a picture or movie. Others talk to themselves and describe the movie. Some get the sensation, for example, as if they were actually walking on the soft warm sand of the beach. They feel the breeze, the sun rays, the presence of other people, and so on.

The way you employ your fantasy does not matter really. The important thing is to use it. Fantasy or imagination is what your inner artist deploys to be creative. So, imagination seems to be the most important instrument of your creativity.

Visualising, therefore, means the mental creation of scenarios, events and human relations through your sight, hearing, self-talk, and body sensations.[1]

Now let us exert our abilities to create a new world through our internal senses.

1- Sit down in a comfortable chair. Breathe deeply several times until your muscles become relaxed. Close your eyes if you want to.

2- Remember the best natural scenery you have ever seen. Describe to yourselves what you can see, hear and feel in that beautiful place.

3- Use the visual submodalities—size, colour, brightness, closeness, location—to specify what you are looking at.

4- Listen again to the sounds you heard in that wonderful scenery. Use the auditory submodalities—volume, tone, tempo, rhythm, location—to make the sounds more alive.

5- Feel again the pleasant body sensations you experienced in that spot. Use the kinesthetic submodalities—body areas where

---

[1] S.Gawain, *Creative Visualization*, New York, NY: Bantam, 1982.

you have a specific sensation, texture, intensity, duration, temperature— to intensify the pleasure.

6- Now describe the countryside, towns, streets, traffic, parks, houses and human relationships that would be like a new paradise for all people.

7- Before you open your eyes, breathe deeply several times. Slowly, move your fingers, hands, arms, shoulders, neck, head, feet and legs. Feel cheerful and optimistic. Open your eyes.

8- Share with another person or with your group the experience of visualising. Clarify your doubts and find out your personal way to use your imagination. According to Albert Einstein, "imagination is more important than knowledge" for scientific progress.[2]

B- *The Practice of Hope*

In this exercise I will integrate the four elements of hope. But I would like to emphasise the basic importance of the *reason* for our hope. We may trust in cosmic energy and the positive trend of life to expect a better future. Or we might trust in humankind to await a better world.

According to the Bible, however, the only one who deserves our complete hope is the Creator. The prophet Jeremiah writes:

"Yahweh says this,
'Accursed be anyone who trusts in human beings,
who relies on human strength
and whose heart turns from Yahweh...'
'Blessed is anyone who trusts in Yahweh,
with Yahweh for his reliance.
He is like a tree by the stream:

---

[2] Cf.R.B.Dilts, *Strategies of Genius II: Albert Einstein.* Capitola, CA: Meta Publications, 1994.

when the heat comes it has nothing to fear,
its foliage stays green;
untroubled in a year of drought,
it never stops bearing fruit'" (17:5-8).

On the other hand, the Creator reveals himself full of love for each of us and for all humankind. Furthermore, He has given us a creative identity and, therefore, He is the source of our orginality and uniqueness. He is able to enhance our creativity as nobody else.

If you are not a believer, however, you can rely on cosmic wisdom, on systemic forces—as Gregory Bateson used to say—, on life, or on human spirit. Ernst Bloch, the Marxist philosopher who studied the social value of hope, based his hope on matter and evolution. And he believed that religion is socially beneficial because it feeds hope in people. He was convinced that people are driven towards utopia by the strength of hope. And he concluded that neither progress nor human history are possible without hope.

The state of hope is fundamental for creating a better future. With hope you are able to act and make the changes that take you, your group, your country and humankind towards progress, justice, peace and happiness.

Let us take action. Living in a continuous state of hope is a habit that must be nurtured through repetitious acts of hope.

1- Take a comfortable body posture. Breathe deeply five times. Pay attention to the inhaling and exhaling of air. Feel the progressive relaxation of your body.

2- Visualise yourselves in the future as being able to express the originality and uniqueness of your own identity. Not only that, observe yourselves expressing your originality for the good of other people, for the benefit of your country and all humankind.

3- If you feel that this is an impossible dream, search immediately for God's face or call on life which is energy: pure creative energy. Trusting in the Creator of life and/or in life, take courage and visualise yourselves being totally creative. Invent a nice story of yourselves being original, creative and beneficial for all people around the world.

4- Use all your senses, if possible, to create that story of your future creativity. In case you cannot see internal images, describe the visual part of the story with words.

5- Watch the movie of your creative service to humankind or listen again to the story. Be sure that it satisfies your better dreams and desires. If not, introduce changes, refine the details, make it perfect.

6- Once you feel satisfied with your own performance, talk to God and express your hope to Him (or to Life): "Lord, I see, hear and feel myself being original, creative and able to contribute to creating a better world for all people, because I trust in You, I hope in You. Since I hope in You, I will do my best to achieve my dream of being unique, creative, and beneficial for everyone."

7- Now, feeling you can achieve your dream, allow yourselves to experience pleasure. Feel the joy of visualising a better future either for yourselves or for other people. Feel ready to take action.

8- Close the exercise with a summary of the steps we follow when we have hope: 1) visualisation of a better future, 2) trusting in God (and/or Life), 3) enjoying the future changes, 4) and feeling ready to take action in order to achieve the dream.

9- Before you open your eyes, breathe deeply several times. Slowly, move your fingers, hands, arms, shoulders, neck, head, feet, legs. Feel your hearts filled with joy, optimism and hope. Continue breathing deeply. Feel the energy of the oxygen you are taking in. Now, open your eyes.

I insist that creativity requires the habit of hope. If you want to awaken your inner artist and allow the expression of his/her originality and creativity, it is necessary to become people of hope. Without hope, an architect would not dream the beautiful lines of a new house. Without hope a leader would not organise the activities of his group. Without hope, a physician would not treat his patients.

2. A PLACE TO DREAM

Perhaps you already know the environment where you are able to dream. You probably know a place where you get better ideas, good solutions, dreams of change and improvement. If not, you are going to discover it.

Robert Dilts suggests, for instance, that Walt Disney had a specific place to dream, another one to transform the dream into action, and a third one to criticise his movies from the financial point of view.

Albert Einstein is quoted as asking, "Why is it I get my best ideas in the morning while I'm shaving?"[4]

If you have not discovered yet where to dream, pay attention to your daily routine and find out your dreaming place. You can also explore different places which you intuitively think could be an appropriate place to dream.

To help you find your best creative spot, do the following exercise.

1- Remember one of the games or sports that gives or used to give you the most pleasure. Recall the feelings of excitement you experienced before starting such a game or sport. Revive the sensations of stimulation and fascination. See yourselves ready to start and to enjoy the incredible fun you derive from that sport. Listen to the voices of your friends, their laughing and shouting.

---

[4] Cf. M.Ray & R.Myers, *Creativity in Business.* New York, NY: Doubleday, 1989, p. 137.

2- Take a group decision of where and how, within this compound or in this building, you will search for a place to dream.

3- Go through all the different rooms, areas and spaces in this compound. Wherever you feel comfortable, try to dream, and to have great ideas.

4- After a time of exploration, discover the most stimulating place for dreaming. Time permitting, go back to your best spot and visualise yourselves creating your own life and adding value to other people's lives.

5- Share your discoveries with your group or with somebody else.

If you are making this creative journey by yourself or with your own family, explore the different possibilities you have at home. Search for the best spot you have to be a dreamer. Physically verify the stimulating qualities of that place. Go there and dream.

3. EMOTIONAL STATE OF CREATIVE DREAMING

You certainly have a specific physical and emotional state when you dream creatively. Most people and creativity researchers agree on this point. They even agree on being able to describe some traits of such a dreaming state. Of course, it presents different characteristics in each person. However, most people agree that it is easier to dream when you have:

1) certain body and mind relaxation
2) feelings of freedom
3) a kind of detachment regarding the results
4) trust and certainty
5) fun and pleasure

For instance, Nolan Bushnell, founder of the Atari company, got the idea for what became a best-selling video game while idly flicking sand on a beach. The chemist Friedrich Kekulé discovered the elusive structure of the benzene molecule while he was relaxing in front of a fire.[5]

I do not mean that creativity does not require effort and work. Far from it. You need effort, discipline, perseverance. And you will deploy your resources to create that dreaming state. Even under pressure, you are able to relax and focus on the best and most beautiful aspects of your reality. Then you will be ready to dream and create good and beautiful things that add value to people's lives.

Know that your state of dreaming spawns the condition to be creative: the intrinsic need to create.

In such an empowering state, you experience the urge to do something for the pure pleasure of doing it rather than for any prize or compensation.

Walt Disney offers a good example of that state. His dreams were not motivated externally by money or any other compensation. He confessed, "money—or rather the lack of it to carry out my ideas—may worry me, but it does not excite me. Ideas excite me."[6]

So, the step you are going to take today is the reinforcement of your ability to enter a dreaming state. Hopefully, you will become able to live permanently in that state. Perhaps you already live an artistic life by remaining in such a state. However, some of you might require personal training to develop the skill to elicit a dreaming state.

1- While you are sitting—in this group or elsewhere—try a body posture that, according to Robert Dilts, corresponds to the

[5] D.Goleman, P.Kaufman, M.Ray, *Creative Spirit*. New York, NY: Dutton, 1992, pp. 21, 23.

[6] R.B.Dilts, *Strategies of Genius I*, o.c., p. 168.

dreaming state: "Head and eyes up. Posture symmetrical and relaxed."[7]

2- Recall one of the most joyful experiences you have ever had in beautiful scenery. See again the beauty of nature in that place. If someone is there with you, look at her/his happy face. Listen to her/his voice, and hear the natural sounds of that site. Feel in your body the sensations of pleasure, delight and happiness. Intensify those feelings and body sensations. One way to intensify your feelings is to make your breathing deep and slow.

3- Now, ask yourselves, "What is good about dreaming creatively?" "Why is there pleasure in dreaming?" Give as many reasons as possible. Discover which one most intensifies your state of joy.

4- Remember that you are creative by nature. You are an image of the eternal Creator. Therefore, you are an artist. Invoke this inner artist or even God in order to feel certain you are capable of dreaming the best of the best. Yes, you can dream the best of the best for others and yourselves.

5- Tell the Creator or at least tell yourselves that you will be happy with the process of dreaming, even though you do not produce a big dream or vision. The goal now is the process of dreaming. The results do not matter really.

6- Imagine a symbol of freedom you can identify with. Perhaps an eagle, a seagull, a saint, an angel, or... Identify with your personal symbol of freedom. Experience an incredible state of no boundaries to your love, creativity and happiness. Nothing and nobody can prevent you from being a perfect image of your Creator. Like Him, you are free to love, to create, and to enjoy the process.

7- Now is the time to take action. Start dreaming. Dream the impossible. Dream the best of the best for people and yourselves.

[7] Ib., p. 189.

46

8- After five or ten minutes of dreaming, talk to your Creator and ask for help and grace to continue dreaming with deep hope in Him.

9- Prepare to end the exercise. Before opening your eyes, breathe deeply several times. Feel the energy produced by the abundance of oxygen. Slowly, move your fingers, hands, arms, shoulders, neck, head, feet and legs. With feelings of freedom, detachment, trust and joy, be ready to open your eyes. Keep breathing deeply. Open your eyes.

10- Share your experience with somebody else or with your group.

4. THE PROCESS OF DREAMING

Before I propose today's step, let me invite you to think of the most beautiful thing in your life just now. Think of the best one as well. Enjoy both of them. Incidentally, I am assuming you have already written your daily pages.

The step you are going to take today is a sort of summary of the last exercises. Simultaneously, you will find a new element of the process of dreaming. I will invite you to explore your dream mode and discover your mental *strategy*.

The basic components of any mental strategy are the *representational systems:* seeing, hearing, feeling, smelling and tasting.

Those sensations are comparable to the digits you dial to make a telephone call. The digits are always the same, and go from 0 to 9. Your office telephone number has those and only those digits. But they have a specific sequence. If I change the sequence, I won't get through. I will succeed in calling you only if I dial the digits in the exact sequence of your telephone number.

Your sensations are like numbers. They are the same in all human beings. But when you dream creatively, you use them in a specific sequence. Perhaps you *listen* to a melody first. Then you get the body *sensations* of relaxation and pleasure. Third, you start to *see* a movie about possible solutions and goals, or great ideas might appear. In this case, your *dreaming strategy* is **A-K-V** (Auditory-Kinesthetic-Visual). It means that you are stimulated by the sound of music (**A**), then you have responsive body sensations (**K**). Finally, you start to produce images (**V**).

Walt Disney described his strategy in the following sentences:

> "We take music and visualize the stories and pictures which the music suggests to imaginations. It is like seeing a concert."
> "When I heard the music it made pictures in my head... here are the pictures."[8]

Now you can discover the sequence of the representational systems in Disney's strategy:

1) The music, as external auditory input (**A**), produces
2) internal imagery (**V**). Later on, Disney would
3) transform these fantasies into external images (**V**) through the process of animation.

Now, what is your personal strategy when you dream creatively?

1- Take a comfortable body posture. Breathe deeply several times. Adopt the dreaming posture: symmetrical and relaxed. Head and eyes up.

2- Recall the last time when you were able to produce creative dreaming. Repeat the same steps you followed during that dreaming process:

1- What was the very first thing you experienced?:

  a- Something you saw?

[8] Ib., p. 166.

b- Something you heard?
c- Something you felt?

2- What was the second thing?:

a- Something you saw?
b- Something you heard?
c- Something you felt?

3- What was the third thing?:

a- Something you saw?
b- Something you heard?
c- Something you felt?

4- What was the fourth thing?:

a- Something you saw?
b- Something you heard?
c- Something you felt?

5- What was the fifth thing?:

a- Something you saw?
b- Something you heard?
c- Something you felt?

Following the same order to these questions, put your answers in a sequence. You will have your own strategy. Let us say that it is something like: 1- something you saw, 2- something you felt, 3- something you heard, 4- something you saw, and 5- something you felt. Then your strategy was: **V-K-A-V-K.**

Suppose you saw the immense blue of the sea. Then you felt relaxed and glad. After that, you visualised a scene in which you expressed your love and tenderness to your loved ones in a special manner. And you heard their voices of gratitude and their expressions of love for you. Finally, you felt the need to meet your loved ones and manifest your love for them.

3- If you think you never had a creative dream repeat yesterday's exercise. Try different ways of doing it, until you are able to produce creative dreams. Afterwards find out your mental strategy.

4- Once you have clarified your *dreaming strategy,* adopt the dreaming physiology: symmetrical and relaxed body posture. Head and eyes up. Once you feel the emotional state of dreaming follow your same strategic steps. As if you were dialing a specific phone number. But this time try to dream the best of the best both for other people and for yourselves.

5- Notice the results. Does your strategy really work? If it works, where and when could you continue using it? In which situations might it not work? If it does not work, what else could you do?

6- Share the results of this exercise with another person or with your group. Use their feedback for further clarification of your personal strategy for creative dreaming.

5. GROUP DREAMING

The possibility of creatively dreaming in a group adds a new element to our creative process. I am not saying that group dreaming will take the place of personal creativity. Not at all. However, working in a group gives you greater scope for exploration, stimulation, feedback, discovery, and so on.

After a productive session of group dreaming, you may go back home with more ideas, with clearer, better ideas.

I recognise that creativity is a personal phenomenon. Simultaneously, I believe that we need changes in our society. And these changes—justice, peace, work, health, freedom, fraternity for each and every person require small groups and communities.

In fact, we are speaking now of learning organisations, learning groups, learning communities. Since the advent of this second half of the twentieth century, we have rediscovered the powerful potential deployed by small groups.

The creation of the world we all want to belong to, will be the fruit of personal, group, organisational, national and international creativity.

So, in the spirit of learning organisations and communities, we are expected to dream in a group. A company anxious to progress through a group learning process, sooner or later will require group dreaming techniques like this.

If you are making this creative journey by yourself, I mean individually, try to create at least the smallest group of two. With your spouse, partner, friend or colleague, you may try this technique of group dreaming.

It would be nice if all the members of this group knew their creative strategy and used it during this exercise. If they don't, it does not matter. They will get great results if they give it all their talent and all their passion.

1- Adopt the dreaming physiology: symmetrical and relaxed body posture. Head and eyes up. Breathe deeply several times.

2- Recall a time when you experienced harmony, collaboration and fun within a small group. Perhaps at home, at school, with your friends, etc. Evoke that experience as vividly as possible. See again what you were seeing during that experience. Hear again what you were hearing. Feel in your body the pleasure you felt. Be ready to enjoy this session of group dreaming.

3- Now produce a dream about the best thing that could happen to humankind.

Use all your senses to describe your dream:

a- Make a picture (Visual).

b- Tell a story (Auditory).

c- Include action and interaction (Kinesthesic).

d- Add, at least in the story, olfactory and gustatory elements.

4- One or more persons—according to the number of participants—will be in charge of the visual system. They will include the visual submodalities in the picture—size, colour, brightness, etc.

5- Another person or persons will be in charge of the auditory quality of the story about the picture or about the dream itself. Perhaps background music might be added. What are the submodalities in the storyteller's voice—volume, tone, tempo, rhythm, etc.?

6- A person or persons will be responsible for the kinesthetic aspect of the dream. This person will ask, for example, "What kind of feelings are required by this dream?" "What body response and feelings are we provoking in other people with our dream?" "What actions or interactions could be introduced in the presentation of our dream?"

7- One or more people will be in charge of the olfactory and gustatory elements of the dream. They will ask the others, "What odours could be involved in our dream?" "What is the taste of our dream?" "Do we like its taste?" "Could we include external things that give taste and odour to our dream?"

8- Once the dream is enriched with all the representational systems, the group decides the last details for the presentation of their dream.

9- Sharing of the group dream.

6. IN CONTEXT WITH LIFE

From a systemic perspective, one characteristic of a good dream is the ecology of it. When we human beings forget our Mother

Nature or Life, we start to destroy our own house which is the Earth.

One of Grinder and Bandler's mentors while they were creating NLP, was Gregory Bateson. He instilled in them a deep concern about the need of a systemic approach to our goals, purposes and dreams. We need to take into account our environment, humankind, nature. If you need heat at home during winter time, you do not kindle a fire on the floor of your drawing room. No. You consider the characteristics of your house and light the fire in the fireplace, to avoid the house catching fire.

But many of us, up to now, do not realise the systemic conditions of our existence. Especially during this century we have contaminated and destroyed our planet as never before. Bateson says:

"Man, after all, has acted according to what he thought was common sense and now he finds himself in a mess. He does not quite know what caused the mess and he feels that what has happened is somehow unfair. He still does not see himself as part of the system in which the mess exists, and he either blames the rest of the system or he blames himself."[9]

Therefore, let us be conscious of the system we live in. Nature or life is a fantastic womb where we all live. Therefore, our dreams must dovetail with life. We are expected to check the ecology of our dreams and goals not only today, but always.

Let us compare our own dream about people, knowing that we are one of them, with some aspects of life.

1- Take a comfortable body posture. Breathe deeply several times. Explore your present environment and discover the best

---

[9] G.Bateson, *Steps to an Ecology of Mind*. New York, NY: Ballantine, 1985, p. 436.

thing and the most beautiful thing present. Enjoy these two aspects of reality.

2- Examine your dream and check if it is open to the torrent of creative energy that characterises life. Is your dream able to communicate with life, to be infused by life's energy, and to enhance life? If your dream receives life's sap, it will grow, it will yield much fruit, and it will last.

3- Life has different habits or trends that yesterday's biologists used to call "laws." Some of those habits are:

a- System-Structure
b- Temporality-Dynamism
c- Self-preservation-Self-repair
d- Communication-Complementation
e- Growth-Self-renewal
f- Differentiation-Gestalt
g- Flexibility-Plasticity
h- Reproduction-Evolution
i- Autonomy-Freedom

Take one or two habits and compare your dream with them. Let us take, for example the growth habit. Life has a natural capability and energy that allows it to grow, and to grow. Growing is natural in any living creature. Is your goal able to grow and evolve together with life?

Machines—cars, computers, radios, etc.—do not have these characteristics. Therefore, is your dream life-like or machine-like?

Later on, when you have time, compare your dream with most of these life habits.[10]

4- Check if your dream is ecological. Does it respect life in all its manifestations—air, water, plants, animals, human beings?

---

[10] Cf.L.J.González, *Psychology of Personal Excellence*. Monterrey, Mexico: Font, 1993, pp. 64-66. F.Capra, *The Turning Point*. New York, NY: Bantam, 1988, pp. 265-304.

Is your dream socially ecological? Does it respect other people's rights, health, development and highest dreams?

5- Introduce in your dream the elements that make it more open to life's creative energy, more similar to life itself, and more ecologic.

6- Share with another person or group this check-up of your group dream.

7. IN HARMONY WITH OUR CREATOR

When Jesus was preaching the good news, he described himself as the source of life, of better and abundant life. He said, "I have come so that they may have life and have it to its full" (Jn 10:10).

And talking about God his Father, Jesus adds, "He is God, not of the dead, but of the living" (Mt 22:33).

God created man, life and everything through his Son, Jesus Christ—according to Christian faith. According to other religions, God's creation happened in a different way. But most of them believe that God is the Creator of everything, especially of life and people.

Through his creation, God reveals himself benevolent, all-powerful, wise, infinite, eternal, increate beauty, etc. The Bible takes for granted that creation shows the attributes of God's perfection.

"Yes, naturally stupid are all who are unaware of God, and who, from good things seen, have not been able to discover Him-who-is, or, by studying the works, have not recognised the Artificer. Fire, however, or wind, or the swift air, the sphere of the stars, impetuous water, heaven's lamps, are what they have held to be the gods who govern the world.

If, charmed by their beauty, they have taken these for gods, let them know how much the Master of these excels them, since it was the very source of beauty that created them.

And if they have been impressed by their power and energy, let them deduce from these how much mightier is He that has formed them, since through the grandeur and beauty of creatures we may, by analogy, contemplate their Author" (Ws 13:1-5).

In a few words, the best of the best that we see, hear, feel, smell and taste in this world, is the expression of God's love. When we pace the goodness of nature, its beauty, and its systemic promotion of life, we are in harmony with the Creator of everything.

When we care for nature and protect its integrity, when we practice justice, keep peace, and love each other, when we accomplish God's commandments, we accomplish His will.

The accomplishment of God's loving will is a specific way to live in harmony with Him. In Jesus' prayer, we adopt a systemic attitude and we agree to pursue our dreams and goals in harmony with God, with nature, with others, and also with ourselves:

"Our Father in heaven,
may your name be held holy,
your kingdom come,
your will be done,
on earth as in heaven..." (Mt 6:9-10).

In order to produce the best dreams for our world, humankind, our people, our company, and so on, we require that cosmic and systemic perspective of the Lord's prayer. Our best dreams take into account God's point of view that includes both heaven and earth. I would say that God cares for the wholeness of His creation. Therefore, when we adopt His perspective and achieve His will, we are dreaming together with Him.

1- Sitting down, adopt the dreaming physiology: symmetrical and relaxed body posture. Head and eyes up. Breathe deeply several times.

2- Acknowledge the presence of the Author of the beauty and grandeur of Creation. With feelings of love and adoration, repeat to Him during three or four minutes: "Our Father in heaven." "Our Father in heaven." "Our Father in heaven."

3- Keeping your eyes closed, and guided by God's own Spirit, use your faith and imagination to see creation through our Father's eyes. Watch the universe, our solar system, our planet, our international society, your nation, your company, your family, yourselves.

4- Through God's eyes look at your group's dream. From this perspective of God's ask yourselves, "Does our dream fit in the wonderful beauty, harmony and goodness of the universe?" Explore as much as possible, through God's eyes, the appropriateness of your dream within the whole of creation.

5- With feelings of infinite peace and joy, leave God's perspective and come back to your own. Using *1st, 2nd* and *3rd positions* examine whether your dream accomplishes God's will. God's will is justice, peace, fraternity, love, systemic harmony, and so on.

6- If you have found some details and refinements that make your dream agree more with God's will, keep them in mind clearly. Be ready to share them with your companions.

7- Before you open your eyes, breathe deeply. Little by little move your fingers, hands, arms, shoulders, neck, head, feet and legs. Feeling more energy because of your deep breathing, open your eyes.

8- Share with your group or with another person what you experienced as you looked at your dream from God's perspective and through his eyes. Mention the suggestions you have now to improve the ecology of your dream.

With this exercise we finish the second week of our creative journey. I am presuming that you continue to write your daily pages. I am sure also of your perseverance in asking yourselves about the best thing and the most beautiful thing present before you at each moment of the day.

And I take for granted that you continue using the creative skills you have exerted during these two weeks.

III- NEW IDEAS THROUGH SYSTEMIC THINKING

Let us presuppose that you feel the *need* of being creative. Then let us take for granted that you have experienced the pleasure of *creative dreaming*. So, you are ready now to produce *new ideas* not only to actualise your dreams, but also to solve your daily problems and to make the most of your possibilities.

I will suggest the new way of thinking, i.e. *systemic thinking* as a means to release new ideas in your daily life. Do not forget, you are an artist. Therefore, you need a creative life in order to be the person you potentially are.

Creativity, let me insist once more, is not a luxury, but one essential aspect of your being. You really need to be creative in order to be yourselves.

You may wonder what the relationship between creativity and systemic thinking is. And my answer is that both walk hand-in-hand. They are complementary.

Systemic thinking represents the ability to see the forest and the trees at the same time. When you look at your family as a whole, instead of just seeing individuals who live together, you are using systemic thinking.

This new way of thinking has actually been used by great people throughout human history. Before, however, it was a kind of privilege of exceptional minds. Nowadays it is becoming more popular. In fact, *systemic thinking* encourages a shift of mind in people. And such a change of mentality involves, at least:

— seeing systems or wholes rather than parts or individuals,
— seeing interrelationships rather than linear cause-effect chains,

— seeing processes of change rather than snapshots.[1]

You can imagine that this way of looking at things seems too vast and therefore rather vague. Nevertheless, it is dynamic, wide, and divergent. These qualities, actually, make systemic thinking apt to be associated with creativity. As soon as you use this way of thinking, you start to be creative.

1. THINKING ABOUT THINKING

To think about thinking is one of the specific tasks that NLP has undertaken. "Richard Bandler has even gone to the trouble to demonstrate, for example, that mathematics is a behavioural science. That may sound odd, but NLP transcends the abstract symbols of math to arrive at the thinking and symbolic processes of the mind. In part at least, NLP is the science of thinking about thinking."[2]

Gregory Bateson, with his own research on human thinking, has encouraged Grinder and Bandler to develop this new branch of science.

They have observed our natural inclination to avoid thinking. We use words and labels to describe things, situations, behaviours, attitudes, without taking the opportunity to ask some further questions about what we are seeing or hearing. We see a red face, wild-eyed, with certain grimaces, and we immediately conclude that a person is *angry*. That's it.

NLP has different techniques to take us out from the pit of mental laziness. In effect, it is said that we produce about 60,000 thoughts each day. But we keep having the same ideas every day.

[1] Cf. G.Bateson, *Mind and Nature: A Necessary Unity*. New York, NY: Bantam, 1988. P.M.Senge, *The Fifth Discipline*. New York, NY: Doubleday, 1990.
[2] J.Yeager, *Thinking About Thinking*. Cupertino, CA: Meta Publications, 1985, p. viii.

Of course, our mental laziness is also very important in daily life. We require clear maps of reality in order to keep ourselves quiet and healthy. We need labels to describe the different phenomena of our world to get orientated within it. We long for quick explanations of people's behaviour, which we summarise in a few words, in order to know how to cope with them.

This way of thinking, which we could call *convergent,* limits our possibilities very often. Most of us have learnt this style of thinking at school. We were supposed to find out an expected solution, just one possible response, the right one. Undoubtedly, up to now we continue thinking like that.

Creative thinking, however, is *divergent.* It produces different hypotheses, adopts different perspectives, asks further questions, produces many ideas.

As you may imagine, both systemic thinking and creativity are stimulants of divergent thinking. However, they do not reject convergent thinking. We need the latter after we have taken a systemic perspective to discover the interrelationships within a system. We need convergent thinking after we have generated several hypotheses and many ideas. Through our convergent thinking we integrate our observations, analyse them, and arrive at conclusions.

Let us practise some exercises that offer the opportunity of using divergent thinking.

1- Search for a place conducive to group or personal creativity.

2- Take a comfortable body posture. Breathe deeply several times. Discover what is good and what is beautiful around you.

3- Explore your way of thinking. Note whether you employ *convergent* thinking too quickly, and *divergent* thinking too rarely.

4- Foresee specific strategies to *diverge* more frequently and effectively in your daily thinking. On the other hand, note which strategies will help you hold back a little on convergent thinking.

5- See yourselves using those strategies in the future: where?, when?, what?, how?

6- Share the results of the exercise with another person or with your group.

The following exercise is very simple. You may do it here and now. But it can be practised everywhere and always. The gist is to come up with ideas you never had before.

The exercise will be more effective carried out within a group—family, learning community, work team, etc.

1- Search for a place where you may feel encouraged to be creative.

2- Take a relaxed and energised body posture. Breathe deeply. Enjoy what is good and what is beautiful at this very moment.

3- Examine your thinking and note whether you tend to prefer:

        a- Vision
        b- Action
        c- Logic
        d- Emotion

4- Once you have discovered your habitual way of thinking, share your discovery with your group or with another person. Give examples to explain your thinking preference.

5- Challenge the beliefs of each person about their thinking: Raise hypotheses, possibilities, doubts that provoke a further exploration in each of you.

6- Think about the possibility of changing your thinking according to the circumstances. Perhaps you may prefer *vision* when you are creating. *Emotional* thoughts might be more appropriate when you watch beautiful scenery. *Logic* may be useful when you summarise a brain-storming session. Thinking in terms of *action* or through certain activities may be ideal when you plan how to train the new employees of your company.

7- Share with others your possibilities to think in different ways. Be concrete and tell how specifically you are going to use the different kinds of thinking. As you listen to your own voice, try to see yourselves accomplishing those possibilities. Be open to the new ideas that will come to your mind while you are speaking.

2. CREATIVE VALUE OF QUESTIONS

I have mentioned that convergent thinking avoids asking further questions. Ready to criticise, it rejects new ideas and daring opinions. As a result, convergent thinking limits its field of exploration. If someone says, "90% of the interviewed doctors recommend this medication," you probably won't raise any objection. You were trained to converge too soon without asking questions about the issue.

Questions play an important role in human creativity. If you decide to be the artist you really are, you will experience a profound tendency to ask more and more questions. Of course, the method of asking questions is an art. You will ask them at the proper time.

Questions have different values. Among them, you may consider the following:

a- Questions change our perspective
b- Questions widen our vision
c- Questions awaken our resources

These three characteristics have a positive influence in our creativity. The last one, however, is the most related with our creativity. The second one is useful to improve our systemic thinking. If you ask yourselves, "What's the picture of my family as a whole?," you will help your mind to widen its perspective.

The first question, on the other hand, is more connected with divergent thinking. If you ask yourselves, "What is the best aspect of reality here and now?," you are changing your perspective.

There are specific questions which might urge your creative resources to take action. They are simple. Nevertheless, they are effective if you keep asking them on a consistent basis.

— What can I do?
— How can I do it?
— What is the best way to do it?
— How can I do it more beautifully?
— What can I do for them—family, group, company, etc.?
— What is really the problem?
— What do I want instead of the problem?
— What is the process to solve the problem?
— Which solutions may I offer?
— What are the best solutions?
— How can I turn this around?
— How could I change the situation?
— How could I improve?
-- How can I live a creative life?
— How can I be the artist I really am?
— How can I increase the beauty of my environment?

After reading these examples, ask yourselves some of them. Choose those you actually need at present. Try answers for those which will help you now. It is better if you do this exercise with somebody else. Your companions could ask you these or similar questions.

After this experience, it is easier for you to understand other qualities of creative questioning. If you ask yourselves, "What is a question?," your brain will start using its resources, and it will offer you answers like:

— A question opens a horizon.
— A question demands an answer.
— A question specifies the coming answer.
— An empowering question yields an empowering answer.
— A question opens the path of creation.
— A question presupposes talents.
— A question awakens the inner artist.
— A question starts a process.
— A question is an adventure.
— A question enhances life.
— A question wants a playmate.

You can use questions not only to open the creative process, but also to close it. At night before you fall asleep, ask yourselves:

— What has been my best experience today?
— What is the best thing I have seen, heard, or felt?
— What is the most beautiful thing I have seen, heard, or felt?
— What did I learn today?
— What was my best contribution to people's well-being?
— What am I grateful for?

At the end of the week, you may review your creative lifestyle during the past seven days.

— This week who has inspired me to be an artist?
— This week have I been the artist I really am?
— This week why have I been more creative or less than before?
— This week how did I manage to be creative?
— This week what were my most creative achievements?
— This week when—day, at what time—have I been creative?
— This week where have I been more creative?

Introduction

Q. Which problem would I like to creatively solve today?
A. I'd like to (write a poem, face my boss...) _____
Q. What specifically makes it a problem? _____

The Questions

1- What is my GOAL?
   a- What is the purpose of my goal or solution?
   b- What is the purpose of that purpose?
   c- What is my final purpose or dream?
   d- What is the real situation just now?

2- Who else is involved in the problem and mainly in the solution?

3- Who am I while searching for solutions?

4- Why is it important to arrive at the best solution?

5- How am I contributing to create the problem?

6- How can I enjoy the process of solving the problem?

7- What is good or even great in this problem?

8- What am I going to do in order to implement the solution?

9- What am I willing to avoid in order to get my goal?

10- Where and when will I take action?

11- How will I know that I am getting closer to the solution?

12- What will I do if I do not get the results I want?

3. USE BOTH BRAINS

Some authors used to say that creativity belonged to our right brain. In fact, NLP has evidence about the special role played by our right brain in certain creative activities. For example, when you construct new images, you will probably raise your eyes up. Furthermore, you will look up to your right to activate your right brain in order to create an image you have never seen.

Even though our right brain seems to play a major role in our creative processes, we believe now that the whole brain is involved in human creativity.

In the early 1960s Roger Sperry and his colleagues did several experiments with split-brain patients—individuals whose connection between brain hemispheres had been altered to decrease the effects of epilepsy.

They confirmed that the two sides of the brain perform different functions. The left side—which controls the right side of the body—seems specialised mainly in language, logic and time; the right side mainly in visualisation, intuition and spatial orientation.

Other studies highlight different layers in our brains. Visualise the human brain: Its hemispheres constitute the *neocortex*—at the very top. Underneath lies the top of the limbic system. This is older than the neocortex, and it is called the *mammalian brain* because we share it with horses, kangaroos, rabbits, rats. It appears to be the source of our needs (drives), feelings, long-term memory, kinesthetic learning, basic social connections.

The brain stem just below known as the *reptilian brain,* and which we share with such reptiles as crocodiles and snakes, is called the primitive brain. It is responsible for the vital drives, the instinctive mechanisms, and the spontaneous reflexes. The survival mechanisms belong to it.

In brief, the creativity of our inner artist requires both hemispheres of our *cortical brain,* the needs and feelings of the *limbic brain,* and the survival mechanisms of the *primitive brain.*

CORTICAL BRAIN	
LEFT - CORTICAL	**RIGHT - CORTICAL**
Logic	Visual
Analytic	Synthetic
Mathematic	Artistic
Concrete	Diffuse
Linear	Holistic
Verbal	Nonverbal
FUNCTIONS	**FUNCTIONS**
Goal-oriented	Intuitive
Conservative	Playful
Planning	Emotional
Organised	Musical
Active	Spiritual
LEFT - LIMBIC	**RIGHT - LIMBIC**
LIMBIC BRAIN	

A- Brain Shifts

Left to Right

1- Visualising, daydreaming
2- discovering patterns, big picture, connections
3- opening up to "irrelevancies"
4- responding to body language, tone of voice, hug, smile, laugh
5- talking to yourself in a positive, supportive way; using colourful, playful, childlike language
6- seeing through others' eyes, trying to feel their point of view
7- moving, exercising, recreating, experiencing, playing, enjoying
8- shifting phone to your left ear (controlled by your right brain) for *empathic* listening
9- doodling, drawing, printing

10- singing rounds, humming, joking, chuckling
11- breathing deeply, saying or thinking "maaa" each time you exhale; doing this until you feel relaxed; taking a stroll to no place in particular

12- carrying a clipboard, notes or other comfort symbol

13- taking a minivacation at your desk; leaning back, relaxing, closing eyes, daydreaming
14- visualising green for freedom to glide, experience, enjoy, soar
15- making eye contact with others to feel their point of view

Right to Left

1- Taking notes, writing on flip chart
2- organising, setting priorities for notes, reviewing agenda
3- evaluating, eliminating extraneous ideas, setting goals
4- analysing body language, tone of voice
5- practising your rational opinions and presentations

6- taking practice run, comparing, judging
7- deciding, recalling, questioning progress, goals, time
8- shifting phone to your right ear (controlled by your left brain) for analytic listening
9- writing, outlining, testing, working crossword puzzle, solving math problem
10- asking questions, making puns

11- striding purposefully, touching toes or performing some other calisthenic activity, counting out loud until you have completed prescribed number
12- using dictating machine, picking up pointer or some symbol of authority
13- going off alone, writing memo describing anger, concern, problem
14- thinking amber or yellow to slow down, considering consequences
15- reporting experience to boss or spouse (preplan it with list)

69

16- relating to someone or something you know or have experienced

17- being aware of the colours, space, aromas, sounds, emotions around you

18- seeing the whole situation, how each person and element is related

16- connecting with time, schedule, historic moment; looking at watch; mentally planning trip or day's activities

17- estimating value of your precision, economies, foresight

18- breaking problem into separate parts, revising policies until consistency prevails[3]

B- *Mindmapping*

Mindmapping is a specific technique to think with your whole brain. You will activate both hemispheres of your cortical brain and the limbic brain as well.

I used this technique for the first time in 1989. John Grinder suggested I mindmap the structure of my first book on NLP.

Mindmapping was invented and developed in the early 1970s by Tony Buzan as a tool to help people take notes more effectively. As he applied this tool, he realised that he had discovered a new way to improve this students' thinking skills.

′ Mindmapping provides a systemic means for recording and enhancing the natural flow of the thinking process by creating a "positive feedback loop" between brain and notes. That is why it

[3] This list of shifts was made by J.Wonder & P.Donovan, *Whole-Brain Thinking*. New York, NY: William Morrow, 1984, pp. 60-61. Cf. T.R. Blakeslee, *The Right Brain*. New York, NY: PBJ Books, 1983. P.Russel, *The Brain Book*. New York, NY: Penguin, 1979. R.Ornsteing and R.F.Thompson, *The Amazing Brain*. Boston, MA: Houghton Mifflin Co., 1986. C.Hampden-Turner, *Maps of the Mind*. New York, NY: Macmillan, 1982. D.Chalvin, *Utiliser tout son cerveau*. Paris: ESF Editeur, 1989. D.Chalvin, C.Rubaud, *Utilisez toutes les capacités de votre cerveau*. Paris: ESF Editeur, 1990. L.de Brabandere, A.Mikolajczak, *Le plaisir des idées*. Paris: Dunod, 1994.

may be used to generate new ideas. It is a powerful method to search for solutions.

Mindmapping implies some very simple elements. According to Buzan there are definite benefits gained from each element.[4] Here is what you do:

1) Keep a resourceful state.

2) Place in the centre of a page an image or graphic representation of the idea, goal, problem or information you want to map.

3) Allow your ideas to flow freely without judgment.

4) Use key words to represent ideas.

5) The relative importance of each idea is clearly indicated. More important ideas will be nearer the centre and less important ideas will be near the edge.

6) Connect key-word ideas to the central focus with lines.

7) Print one key word per line.

8) Use colour to highlight and emphasise ideas.

9) Use images and symbols to highlight ideas and stimulate your mind to make other connections.

Have fun now as you draw your own mind map. Just follow the above instructions. I offer you an example that requires colour and more graphics and symbols. Use images instead of words, especially in the centre. If possible, draw a coloured image for the central idea.

[4] T.Buzan, *Make the Most of Your Mind.* New York, NY: Simon & Schuster, 1988. T.Buzan, *Use Both Sides of Your Brain.* New York, NY: Penguin, 1991. J.Wycoff, *Mindmapping.* New York, NY: Berkley Books, 1991. P.Kline & B.Saunders, *Ten Steps to a Learning Organization.* Arlington, VA: Great Ocean, 1993, pp. 166-179.

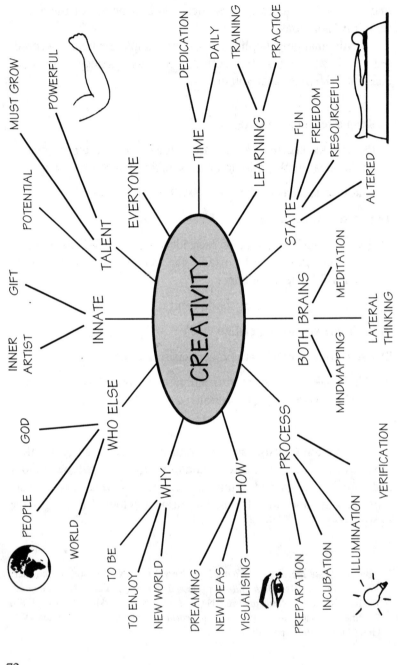

CREATIVITY

MUST GROW
POWERFUL
POTENTIAL
TALENT
EVERYONE
DEDICATION
DAILY
TRAINING
PRACTICE
TIME
LEARNING
FUN
FREEDOM
RESOURCEFUL
STATE
ALTERED
GIFT
INNER ARTIST
INNATE
MEDITATION
BOTH BRAINS
MINDMAPPING
LATERAL THINKING
GOD
WHO ELSE
PEOPLE
WORLD
PROCESS
VERIFICATION
TO BE
TO ENJOY
WHY
NEW WORLD
DREAMING
NEW IDEAS
HOW
VISUALISING
PREPARATION
INCUBATION
ILLUMINATION

4. LATERAL THINKING

Edward de Bono, a psychologist and a doctor in medicine, has developed a specific method which helps your mental development. The method of lateral thinking offers different techniques that make you push yourself to look farther and in different ways.[5]

Vertical thinking, the one we use most of the time, I would say is the same kind of thinking which others call *convergent*. According to De Bono, it has the following characteristics:

— Selective,
— moves only if there is a direction in which to move,
— analytical,
— sequential,
— demands that you be correct at any step,
— criticises in order to block off certain pathways,
— makes you concentrate and exclude what is irrelevant,
— its categories, classifications and labels are fixed,
— follows the most likely paths,
— is a finite or limited process.

Lateral thinking does not exclude the vertical one. Simply, it has different characteristics:

— Generative,
— moves in order to generate a direction,
— provocative,
— can make jumps,
— makes you feel free at any step,
— does not criticise, accepts any kind of possible paths,
— welcomes chance intrusions,
— its categories, classifications and labels are not fixed,

[5] E.de Bono, *Lateral Thinking*. New York, NY: Harper & Row, 1973. E.de Bono, *De Bono's Thinking Course*. New York, NY: Facts On File, 1994.

— explores the least likely paths,
— is probabilistic, i.e. open to infinite possibilities.[6]

NLP, by its very nature, requires lateral thinking. In fact, NLP invites you to continually search for alternatives and to use different perspectives.

A- *In Search of Alternatives*

As soon as you search for alternatives, you start to create new ideas. Certainly, the human mind contains a natural request for alternatives. But the conscious search for alternatives is quite another thing.

The natural search for alternatives inclines you to look for the best possible approach. In the lateral search for alternatives you will try to create as many alternatives as possible. In this case you want to have not just the *best* idea but as many different ideas as possible.

That is why NLP assumes: "The most effective and ecological models are those which produce the widest and richest number of choices, as opposed to being the most 'real' or 'accurate'."

Let us try an exercise for the generation of alternatives. In NLP we use a simple question which you can ask yourself as frequently as possible:

— Which other alternatives do I have?
— What are the choices that I have?
— Which other choices may I offer him/her?
— Although I have the best alternative, which others might be great alternatives?
— How can I generate more alternatives?

---

[6] E.de Bono, *Lateral Thinking*, o.c., pp. 39-45.

Another exercise, which you may do in a group or with another person, requires your lateral thinking.

1- Sitting down, adopt your dreaming physiology: symmetrical and relaxed body posture. Head and eyes up. Breathe deeply several times.

2- Recall a specific person's need you could satisfy, or think of one personal need—painting, writing a poem, improving a relationship, solving a financial problem, etc.

3- Share your problem, need or possibility with your group. Sort out the most common problem or desire, so that all of you may work on it.

4- Imagine that you have agreed to search for solutions for an interpersonal problem. One of you cannot bear a difficult person—a colleague, a neighbour, an adolescent son, etc.

5- Search for alternative solutions. The best way to have good ideas is to have as many as possible. So, at the moment, it is the quantity not the quality what matters.

6- Suspend your judgment. Do not criticise other people's ideas. On the contrary, use their ideas to generate further alternatives.

7- When you have more than twenty alternatives the exercise is over. The group with the largest quota deserves a reward from the main trainers.

A variation of the above exercise is the search for new descriptions for the same object, problem, matter, person, and so on.

1- Take a dreaming physiology. Breathe deeply. Ask yourselves what is the nicest and what is the best thing around yourselves.

2- Find a common situation, problem, or possibility to be creative.

3- Describe that person you have decided to describe. Perhaps it is Jesus of Nazareth. Try as many descriptions of him as possible.

4- This time, note the variety of descriptions. There are as many descriptions as heads present. Thus, an NLP premise says: "Every person has their own individual map of the world... No individual map of the world is more 'real' or 'true' than any other." Experience this fact through the present exercise.

5- Once you acknowledge the variety and diversity of maps, the exercise is over.

The purpose of this exercise is double. The first one is to get accustomed to generating alternatives. The second one is to train you to realise that there is more than one way of looking at a situation. For this reason the emphasis is not on the accuracy of the description but on the *difference* between descriptions and the use of novel methods of description.

B- *A Systemic Lateral Thinking*

NLP, especially through Robert Dilts and the late Todd Epstein, has a systemic way of improving lateral thinking. When you take *perceptual positions, logical levels* and *time frame* at the same time, you will certainly practise your lateral thinking skills.

Try the following steps together with another person or within your group.

1- Elicit a resourceful state. Pay heed to the most beautiful and to the best reality around you. Derive pleasure from them. Remember a time when you were very skillful in performing a task. Revive the thoughts, feelings and body sensations you experienced during such successful activity.

2- Take a problem you want to solve, something you have decided to invent, an image you intend to draw or paint.

3- Specify your goal. Establish *what you really want*.

4- Consider your goal—solutions, invention, piece of art, etc.—from different perspectives and get new ideas from each perspective, i.e:

1st position (ACTOR)
2nd position (PARTNER)
3rd position (OBSERVER)
Transcendental (GOD'S EYES)

5- Jot down your new ideas. Next, explore your goal from different *logical levels,* that is:

Where/When?	ENVIRONMENT
What?	BEHAVIOURS
How?	CAPABILITIES
Why?	BELIEFS/VALUES
Who?	IDENTITY
Who Else?	SPIRITUAL

As you go through the first *Who?,* think of yourselves as creators: Who you really are while you create new ideas for the problem, invention, etc. The *Who Else?* refers to people who will benefit from the solution, or those who will implement the solution, and so on. Of course, the *Who Else?* might make you think of God.

6- You may get more ideas if you consider your goal in a wider *time frame:* past-present-future. Imagine a line, or a scenario, or a big screen where you put: *past* at your left, *present* in front of you, *future* on your right. Study your solution, invention, artistic work, etc. within these three stages of the arrow of time.

PAST   PRESENT   FUTURE

Jot down your new ideas, your discoveries, your observations.

7- If you prefer, use the graph on the next page, which Dilts and Epstein designed to stimulate lateral thinking from the NLP perspective.

8- Share your experience of systemic lateral thinking with another person or with other groups. Enjoy their feedback.

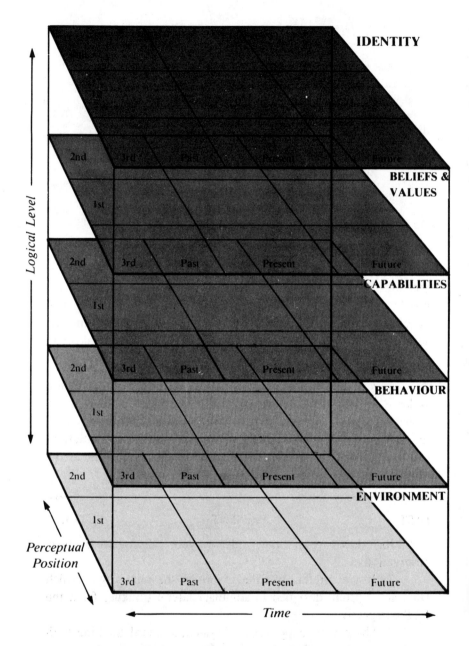

(Robert B. Dilts & Todd Epstein)

5. SYSTEMIC THINKING IN PRACTICE

As you know, through *systemic thinking* our mind sees whole interrelationships and processes of change. And this is your task now: to look for a specific system and discover the interrelations of its different parts and its process of change.

1- Acquire a resourceful state, that is, a state that allows you to have your personal resources available. You may remember a specific experience in such a state. Perhaps you told jokes that provoked spontaneous laughter. Perhaps you prepared a wonderful dish in the kitchen, or you gave good counsel, or you helped somebody in great danger. Revive the thoughts, feelings and body sensations you had during that experience.

2- As you feel in a resourceful state, watch your family, company, church, world, or whatever system you might recall.

3- Now, look at the system—the one you have chosen—as a whole. Use an image to help your mind. See your family as a human body: head, trunk and extremities. But do not pay too much attention to the different parts—who is the head, and who is the heart. See rather the wholeness, the family as a system.

4- Discover what kind of system the wholeness you are studying is. What is its image? What are its characteristics? What is its size, form, age, and so forth.

5- Explore now the relationships within the system. How do the different parts relate to each other? How does each part affect the others? How does each part affect the whole system? What kind of relations do they have among themselves: symmetrical, asymmetrical, complementary?

6- Note, next, what process of change that system is living. Is it a real evolution? Is it in a state of stagnation or even of self-destruction? What are its possibilities of change and improvement? What ideas could you offer for its improvement?

7- Share your global picture, your discoveries and ideas with somebody else or with another group.

Our habitual thought patterns make us see linear cause-effect chains. For example, we say: "She has shouted at me. I feel rejected by her. I prefer to avoid talking to her." Simultaneously, she thinks: "He does not speak to me. I feel rejected by him. So, I will demand an objective explanation of his behaviour."

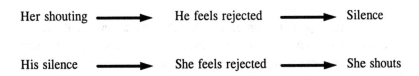

What is really happening between them is a circle of causality. They form a true system. Therefore, they influence each other in a circular way. They are creating a perpetual and increasing cycle of aggression. If they do not come out of their situation to have a look at themselves as a whole, they will divorce in spite of the love they may have for each other. However, if they see themselves as a system, they will realise the following causality circle.

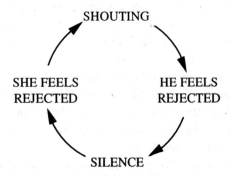

It is necessary that both he and she be aware of the system and that they realise their part in the problem. After that, they have to contribute in order to stop the cycle of mutual aggression.

As you follow the next exercise, you will have the opportunity to transform some of your habitual cause-effect chains into loops of causality.

1- Recall a specific time when you experienced a resourceful state. See what you were seeing; hear what you were hearing, and feel the energy, self-confidence, and your ability to deploy the resources that you felt then. Keep this state all through this exercise.

2- Find common situations that you or others describe as linear cause-effect chains. It will be much better if you recall the two parallel lines which describe the position of a person, group, or nation.

3- Discover how the two straight lines form a circle. Repeat the same procedure with as many situations as possible.

4- Share your experience with another person or with your group.

A sort of extension of the above exercise is the search for systemic causes. You can move from the cause-effect explanation to the "pattern explanation," and from this to a systemic explanation.

Let me give an example taken from the present situation in my country. Since December 1994 Mexico has suffered a severe economic crisis. Most people search for an immediate cause: the rebels of Chiapas, or the death of presidential candidate Luis Donaldo Colosio, or the sudden devaluation of our currency, or economic abuses by the last president.

This is the *cause-effect explanation*. But according to systemic thinking, this way of seeing things is rather superficial. We could take a further step by asking, as few thinkers have done in Mexico, "How many times has the same kind or a similar kind of financial crisis taken place?" Some historians go back to the colonial times.

The answer to this question will show that such crises keep repeating themselves from time to time. They represent a sort of pattern. And when you discover it, you have a *pattern explanation.*

You may go a step further by asking another question: "What is the cause of that pattern?"

When you answer this question you get a *systemic explanation,* which is the most promising and generative. It will suggest the real solution to the problem.

1- Take a comfortable body posture. Concentrate on the best and the most beautiful things just now. Enjoy having both here and now. Move from this pleasant experience to a resourceful state. Remember a time when you felt the availability of your resources. Revive the body sensations of the specific experience you are recalling at this moment. And retain such body sensations during the present exercise.

2- Remember a problem, an experience of being creative, a very happy situation.

3- Find out the *cause-effect explanation* for that event or experience. For example, ask yourself, "What caused my happy experience?"

4- Once you know the immediate cause of the experience or problem, find out how many times and in which circumstances the same experience or the same problem has been present. This way you will find the *pattern explanation.*

5- After you have realised that such a problem has appeared several times in specific circumstances during a certain period of time, ask yourselves, "What is the cause of this pattern?" The answer is the *systemic explanation.*

6- If you are dealing with a problem, produce structural solutions in order to radically solve it. If you are working with a succesful situation or with a happy experience, have a clear idea of the deepest root of your happiness, inspiration or success.

7- Share the results of this exercise.

6. THE WISDOM OF YOUR UNCONSCIOUS MIND

I believe that our intuition, inspiration, presentiments and all sudden expressions of our inner wisdom are manifestations of our unconscious mind. And as I said before, it is deeply connected with our inner artist. Therefore, I consider it very important that we have ways to get in touch with it.

Your unconscious mind is open to your requests and suggestions during the last minutes of your daily journey. Your inner artist smiles at you more openly before you fall asleep. During the night, in your dreams he even speaks to you. For example, Otto Loewi, a Nobel Prize-winner in medicine, discovered the chemical transmission of the nervous impulse while he was sleeping. On Easter night in 1921 he was awakened by an idea. He turned the light on, wrote some notes and fell asleep again. But next day he could not understand his hieroglyphics. That day was the most grievous of all his scientific life. But he was lucky. The following night he got the same idea. He did not run any risk this time. He got up, went to the laboratory and, at five o'clock, the chemical transmission of the nervous impulse was already demonstrated.[7]

When you wake up in the morning, your inner artist opens the door of your innermost core and shows his face to you.

You may get in touch with your inner artist before you fall asleep, during sleep, and as soon as you wake up. Ask for his help. Beg for his wisdom. Request his ideas. Most of all, give him chance to work out the problems, difficulties, and challenges you have in life. As soon as you desire a solution or a good idea, ask him for help. Let him work alone in the deepest and incredibly beautiful core of your soul.

When we allow our inner artist to work on his own, we allow the most important stage of creativity to occur. In fact,

---

[7] Cf. J.Rof Carballo, *Medicina y actividad creadora*. Madrid, Revista de Occidente, 1964, pp. 84-86.

according to some authors, the creativity process has four stages: *preparation, incubation, illumination* and *verification*. The second one, *incubation,* represents the hidden activities of our inner artist.[8] In the secret laboratory of our personal core, our creative self generates new ideas, solutions, artistic inspirations and enlightening intuitions.

Through our reading, reflection, consultations, conversations, creative exercises, and so on, we achieve the first stage, that is, *preparation.* Afterwards, we leave the work in our inner artist's hands.

There are different ways, after the period of preparation, to encourage our inner artist to take action by himself. We can use the time of sleep, the altered states of consciousness, the shifts from left to right brain.

1- State your desired state—goals, solutions, etc.—in clear terms before you go to sleep. Write the objective down or draw it, if possible. Repeat it mentally as if it were a mantra. Even if you forget your dreams, you may get an answer in the morning.

2- When you go to sleep, keep repeating the objective or question to yourself. Pray or meditate as usual, but ask God for help. Make sure you have a paper and pencil next to you. You could even record your dream on a tape recorder immediately upon waking.

3- When you wake up, lie still for a while. Visualise and memorise a crucial detail of your dream. Then record your dream with a minimum of movement.

4- Ask yourself, "What is the answer given by my inner artist through this dream?" "What is he trying to tell me about myself, people, values, resources, activities, places, time?" "If the dream expresses different parts of my being, what does it reveal?"

---

[8] S.Arieti, *Creativity.* New York, NY: Basic Books, 1976. J.Brockman (Ed.) *Creativity.* New York, NY: Simon & Schuster, 1993.

5- Make a drawing or a mind map to picture the message that comes from the dream. Put together both the picture and your description of the dream. Then, ask yourself, "What does all this tell me?"

6- Indulge in a three- or five-minute prayer or meditation. Wait for the inspiration or solution, if you have not got it yet. During the day, perhaps when you are distracted or doing something irrelevant, you will get your inner artist's answer.

The following exercise describes a way to change your mental state. It is a state that opens the door of your being to your inner artist.[9]

1- Take a comfortable body posture. Breathe deeply several times. But this time pay attention to the air that comes and goes with each breath. Hold the air inside during five or ten seconds. Then exhale slowly.

2- Pay attention now to colours and details that you do not normally notice.

3- Be attentive and listen to the different sounds that are present here and now.

4- Be aware of your body position. Feel the parts of the seat that your body is touching. Be conscious of the temperature of your hands and face. Experience the earth attracting your feet. Follow the rhythm of your breathing.

5- Remember now the most enjoyable landscape you have ever seen. See what you saw there. Listen to the sounds characteristic of that place. Feel again the body sensations and feelings you experienced in that beautiful scenery.

6- Imagine now that you are going inside yourself. Discover the beautiful scenery of your innermost core. Meet your inner artist. He is your own identity, the unique you, created in God's image. You cannot imagine all the beauty, value, and power of your real self, i.e. your inner artist. He is infinitely better than

---

[9] J.Grinder and R.Bandler, *Trance-formations*. Moab, Utah: Real People Press, 1981.

what you can perceive in him. Although you cannot capture all the value and power of your real self, admire him and enjoy him.

7- Present your dreams, desires and goals to your inner artist. Ask him for help. Rely on him. Be grateful to him. Express your love for him. Let him work when he wants and in the way he prefers.

8- Leave your interior landscape and come back to your external world. Feel your body relaxed and comfortable. Breathe deeply. Feel the energy and vigour that you are getting each time you breathe. Slowly, move your fingers, hands, arms, shoulders, neck, head, feet, legs. Continue breathing deeply. Be ready to open your eyes. Open your eyes!

9- Share your experience.

You already know the third exercise. Go back to the list of shifts. Move your attention and perceive those aspects of reality that your right brain enjoys: a green meadow surrounded by a dense forest... Beyond this, the white peaks of the mountains that pierce the blue sky and open a skylight to imagine the unlimited happiness of eternity...

While you are using your right brain, in one way or another you are getting in touch with your inner artist. Some specialists in Ericksonian hypnosis consider the unconscious mind equal to the right brain.[10]

7. ILLUMINATION: APPEARANCE OF NEW IDEAS

When you least expect it, your inner artist delivers his inspiration, ideas, solutions. He waits for those moments when your conscious mind is relaxed or sluggish. This happens while you are taking a

---

[10] T.R.Blakeslee, *The Right Brain*, o.c., pp. 20-28. T.Robles, *Concierto para cuatro cerebros*. Mexico: Instituto Milton Erickson, 1990.

shower, walking around, while you are dancing or watching TV, when you wake up, and so on. In those situations, your inner artist makes the most of his opportunity. He outwits the control and critiques of the conscious mind, and offers his illumination.

I do not have any exercise to provoke such illumination. But you can encourage your inner artist to be more active in your daily life by devoting time to special moments of rest, relaxation, aerobic exercise, meditation, quiet or concentrated prayer.

Your inner artist also requires feelings of peace, joy, hope, optimism, love, compassion, service, etc. to feel free to release and express his ideas.

I have another suggestion taken from both my experience as a writer and my therapeutic work: take action. While you are trying to undertake a task which you do not know how to start, the ideas and solutions come in the middle of your trials and errors. Thus, *action itself is a source of creativity.*

IV- CREATIVE ACTION

The *verification* stage that comes after illumination, means to take action. You must transform the illumination—idea, solution, artistic inspiration—into action. You are going to verify whether your idea gets the results you really want.

According to Teresa Amabile, author of the book *The Social Psychology of Creativity,* an idea or product is creative when it is *new, appropriate* and *useful.* How else could you know if your product or ideas meet these conditions but through the verification process?

On the other hand, still according to the same author, creativity contemplates some personal characteristics. One of them is *intrinsic motivation,* that is, the inner need or urge to create something. Such a need, which we have already studied, involves the reptilian and mammalian brain in the creative process. Therefore, we are prone to do something for the sheer pleasure of doing it.

Another characteristic of creative people is what Amabile calls "creative thinking skills." And my last chapter, as you know, is dedicated precisely to those *creative thinking skills.* During the last seven days you have used your thinking skills.

A third characteristic people need to be creative is expertise in a specific area, that is, *domain skills.* You are supposed to know lots of music, certain rules of composition, how to write musical notation, etc. to be a creative composer.

Thus, I presuppose that you have the *domain skills* you require to take action in a creative way. However, there are many secondary areas of your daily life that do not demand much expertise on your part. For instance, you can offer a very creative counsel to your friend without being a psychologist or a counsellor. You may bake a delicious cake without being a professional cook. And so forth.

This fourth stage of our creative journey will offer fewer activities than the last one. I hope you will be able to cover each day's tasks.

1. ANCHORING THE RESOURCEFUL STATE

Most exercises of the previous stages call for a specific emotional state. Remember, emotions and feelings belong to the limbic or mammalian brain. Therefore, as a way to involve the creative resources of this brain, we have to pay heed to our emotional state.

On the other hand, when you are active it is almost impossible for you to sit down, breathe deeply, recall a successful experience, and get a resourceful state. Imagine yourself talking to a client. From your *3rd position* you feel the need to try a different strategy. Are you going to ask your client to wait until you change your state through relaxation, memory and imagination? Of course not, it would be ludicrous!

You need something simpler that can instantly change your state. NLP creators have invented a state-changing procedure which is called *anchoring*.

When you see a face and automatically feel happy, you may say that his/her face is an *anchor* for you. Sometimes you smell a specific perfume and unconsciously feel a sexual arousal. It is clear that perfume became an *anchor* for you. Also you might happen to eat a specific sort of salad and instantly feel humorous. You do not know why. Simply, you are ready to tell jokes. Why? Probably you were eating this kind of salad while you were once experiencing an intense state of joy and good humour.

My favourite example of *anchor* is the traffic lights. They are a sensory stimulus that causes automatic changes in your body. Any sensory stimulus—visual, auditory, kinesthetic, olfactory, gustatory—deserves the name of *anchor* if it changes your body sensations instantly.

The anchoring process implies four stages:

1) Intensity of the emotional state.
2) "Purity" and peak of the state.
3) Uniqueness of the stimulus.
4) Exact replication of the stimulus.

If you follow these steps, you are able to create an *anchor* that triggers the resourceful state whenever you want. You may be arguing with your wife or talking to your boss; if you want to feel resourceful, you will use your *anchor* and change your state. Your anchor, which John Grinder and Judith DeLozier taught me as the "Circle of Excellence," will have you in a resourceful state in a few seconds.

1- Imagine a circle one step in front of you. This circle may have a special colour. Perhaps your "Circle of Excellence" is white, or luminous, or...

This circle can be present everywhere: at home, in your office, in the cinema, at the airport, in your car, in your bed, everywhere. One short step in front of you is enough to enter that empowering circle.

2- Remember an occasion when you were really successful or at least you did a good job of something. Perhaps you told a joke that caused great laughter, or you prepared a delicious meal.

Once you have pictured the occasion, remember what you were looking at. Listen to the sounds that were present during that experience. But, most of all allow yourselves to feel the same sensations of energy, courage, ability. Increase these body sensations by adopting a body posture or a facial expression which fits this resourceful state you are trying to amplify.

3- Hopefully you have reached the "peak" of this resourceful state. I also presuppose that the sensations and feelings of this state are "pure," i.e. all are empowering, and that you do not experience now any uncomfortable or negative sensation.

4- If this is the case, step into your *Circle of Excellence.* Associate this circle with your emotional state of excellence, that is, with your resourceful state. Enjoy having this new tool which endows you with the skill to trigger a resourceful state everywhere and at any time.

5- Step back, out of your circle, and repeat exactly the same procedure. Recall another specific experience which gave you the opportunity to do something well, perhaps very well. Awaken that state, and when it reaches its peak, step into your *Circle of Excellence.*

6- Share your experience.

From today on, whenever you recall a resourceful state, anchor it to your *Circle of Excellence.* If you are living a moment of excellence in your daily activities, immediately link that resourceful state to your circle of light.

On the other hand, whenever you experience the need to feel a state of excellence, just take a step and enter your circle.

When you need all your resources to be creative, then use your *Circle of Excellence*.

2. SYSTEMIC ACTION PLANNING

Suppose you have got an idea about the picture you want to paint, or you have a solution for your problem. The next step, of course, is verification. You will transform the idea into action. You are going to verify if it really works.

But before you take action, you will plan such action. And you plan in a systemic way, so that it is creative.

To do so, follow the circle of the T.O.T.E.:

$$
\begin{aligned}
\textbf{T} &= \text{Test} \\
\textbf{O} &= \text{Operate} \\
\textbf{T} &= \text{Test} \\
\textbf{E} &= \text{Exit}
\end{aligned}
$$

The T.O.T.E. process was discovered by G.Miller, E.Galanter and K.Pribram. It is another way to explain the behaviour in a single event. It is also an extension of the "reflex arc," in the sense that it includes a feedback operation as an intermediate activity between the stimulus and the response. The *Test* represents that intermediate activity to meet certain conditions *before* the response will occur.

You will plan your action according to the T.O.T.E. by answering the following questions:

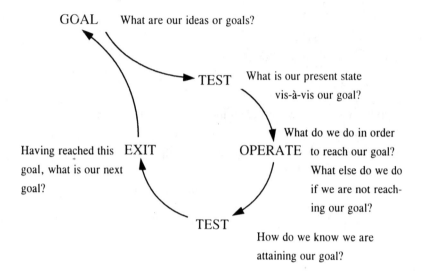

GOAL   What are our ideas or goals?

TEST   What is our present state vis-à-vis our goal?

What do we do in order

EXIT   OPERATE to reach our goal?

Having reached this goal, what is our next goal?   What else do we do if we are not reaching our goal?

TEST

How do we know we are attaining our goal?

Let me give an example. The *goal* of your group is to mindmap a shared vision. First you *test* your present state. You realise that most of the members have some doubts about their vision. So, you *operate* through a brainstorming session in order to get your goal. In effect, ideas become clearer. You are mindmapping.

When the mind map seems to be ready, you make a *test* to check if something is missing. The images and colours are rather poor. Then, you *operate* once again to highlight the main ideas with colour. Simultaneously, more images are used for the same purpose.

You *test* the mind map again. This time you feel satisfied. Therefore, you *exit* from this activity. You are free to undertake the following T.O.T.E. Life, in fact, is an endless chain of T.O.T.E.s.

The following diagram may help to produce a plan geared to the systemic process of a T.O.T.E.

What are my (our) goals?	
What is my (our) present state with regard to my (our) goals?	
What do I (we) do in order to reach my (our) goals?	
How do I (we) know I (we) am (are) attaining my (our) goals?	
What else do I (we) do if I (we) am (are) not reaching my (our) goals?	

Another way to plan systemically is to integrate the *perceptual positions, logical levels* and *time frame*. If these three aspects of reality are present in your planning, you will have a global picture of the action you intend to take.

You have in the first column:

Who Else, i.e. the people who will receive the benefits of your idea or product. It also refers to people involved in the materialisation of your idea.

Who, includes the actors, that is, the person or group who are the creators of that idea and/or want to transform it into action.

Why, here we are at the level of beliefs and values; therefore, it offers an opportunity to clarify the presuppositions, motives, values, purposes included in your idea.

How, at this level of capabilities you may specify the resources and skills required to carry out the idea. And you may extend this item to other practical aspects like equipment (video, flip chart, colours, paper, depending on the area of your creativity), information and control.

What, this level of behaviours refers to the product, service, idea, etc., that you want to materialise. It corresponds, of course, to your goals, outcomes, process and steps. These two, process and steps, could be planned at the level of capabilities if you prefer so.

Where, as you have imagined, is related with house, room, setting, and any other aspect of place. But this category may be widened. You are supposed to consider the context, relations to other systems, situation within the country, continent, planet.

When, this item, in itself, refers to calendar of activities, schedule, duration of meetings, and so forth. However, it is connected with *time frame.*

Time frame, actually, makes you imagine a screen where past, present and future are present as a whole. Therefore, you may plan your action using *past* lessons, realising what is really happening in the *present,* and foreseeing the possibilities of the *future.*

The *perceptual positions* help you to plan from your own perspective (I, we), but also from your partner's and people's perspective (you). You widen the perspective even more when you adopt the observer's position. This position lets you see the interaction and interrelations between you and your partner. Of course, God's perspective is very enlightening.

LOGICAL LEVELS

Logical Levels	Past		You	Others	Present	
Who Else You, Others People, Personnel, etc.			You	Others		
Who I, We, Our Group Our Identity		I (We)				I (W
Why Purposes, Values, Motivation, Beliefs						
How Skills, Equipment, Information, Controls						
What Goals, Outcomes, Process, Steps						
Where Place, Setting, Context, Relation to Other Systems						
When	Past				Present	

TIME

You	Others		I (We)		You	Others	AGENT & PERCEPTUAL POSITIONS
		Future					

3. GROUP ACTION

Now is the time to carry out your plan to transform your idea into action. Write a poem, prepare that food, paint a picture, design a car, try a new teaching method, talk to your partner or start a business.

Here are some suggestions to help you act creatively:

1- *Open your senses.* See objects, forms, colours you do not habitually pay attention to. Listen to sounds you are not normally aware of. Perceive new body sensations and understand the messages your unconscious mind is sending to you through such sensations. Perceive all kinds of smell in yourself, others, the environment. Take time to really taste whatever you eat.

2- *Read in a different way.* John Grinder suggests using only the visual system while reading. Ordinarily we use both visual and auditory systems. If you are not reading technical material or poetry, use only your visual skills.

Read magazines, books and newspapers that you have never read. Discover what is new for you. Examine the originality and beauty of ideas. Be an active reader: underline, use colours, jot down the best ideas.

3- *Watch TV in a new way.* Observe the different perceptual positions in people, emcees, movies, and so on. Search for new channels, study the creativity deployed in advertising, sort out the highest-quality advertising.

4- *Watch the architecture around you.* Enjoy beautiful houses and buildings. If you enter a house that you have not seen before, pay heed to all the details: ceiling, floor, furniture, plants and art objects.

5- *Spend time with children.* Play with them and notice their originality, playfulness, cheerfulness. Go to a park with children. Enjoy their sense of observation, curiosity and admiration.

6- *Do something new within your group.* Ask questions if you usually don't. Challenge other people's affirmations. Express your own feelings. Suggest to them a different perspective, e.g. from *3rd position.*

7- *Be more active in your group.* Offer suggestions. Ask empowering questions; for example, "How could we improve the quality of our best products?" Recall the vision of the group, company, institution, club, etc. Emphasise the real identity of the group: "We are this... not that."

8- *Encourage group creativity.* Ask empowering questions about changes, improvement, excellence. Enhance the use of thinking skills, especially through the search for alternatives. Encourage everyone to learn from errors.

9- *Sharing each other's resources.* Specify the talents and resources of each person in the group. Make a list of each one's good points. Focus on their further possibilities.

The last point deserves a specific exercise. It stimulates group synergy and development. When each member feels appreciated and encouraged to use his/her resources, the group action is spontaneous, creative and full of fun. You could try the following steps.

1- Breathe deeply several times. Be aware of the best and the most beautiful things presently in existence. Derive pleasure from these two aspects of reality. Use the *Circle of Excellence* or any other anchor that triggers your resourceful state.

2- Divide your group. Working just with one other person, with your family, or with a small group, presents no problem. But if your group is too big, form groups of four people.

3- Make a list of resources and skills for each member of the group. A skill means a resource that is not just a potentiality, but an ability you might use here and now. A painter is able to paint your portrait right now, if you want. He already has this skill. But he is also able to paint a landscape even though he has never tried.

Use brainstorming to produce such a list. Each person will mention his proven talents, and others as well. Do not judge any idea that is expressed. The session should be as free-wheeling as possible. Participants are encouraged to hitchhike on the ideas of others. Quantity, not quality of people's resources, is the goal of this particular brainstorming.

4- Select the best resources of each participant. Make a quick plan for the integration of these talents and skills.

5- Take action. Pursue one of your ideas relying on each other's resources.

6- Share the results of this exercise. Highlight what you have learnt through the process of sharing your resources.

4. KEEP YOUR GOAL IN MIND

The most popular version of the T.O.T.E. is what some authors call the summary of NLP:

1- GOAL: Know what you want and keep your outcome clear in any situation.

2- ACTION: Take action. Use your personal power by taking action.

3- ACUITY: Be alert and keep your senses open so that you notice whether you are getting closer to your goal or farther away.

4- FLEXIBILITY: If what you are doing does not get the results you want, be flexible to keep changing until you get what you really want.

This section proposes an exercise for more than just today. It should be a daily exercise. Something like the question, "What is the best and the most beautiful thing here and now?" Yes, to keep a goal in mind in any situation represents one of the best secrets of highly effective people.

In fact, having a clear idea of the outcome in any situation is more than a matter of effectiveness. It has a deeper sense than the practical one.

Knowing what you really want in life means you have a vision both as a person and as a group.

I agree with P.Senge that our dreams and better ideas require special care to remain alive. Several factors may destroy them. When new people join the group and do not assimilate the group vision, it can die. Our dreams frequently wither because we get discouraged. The apparent difficulty in bringing the dream or idea into action makes us quit the action process. As the clarity of our dream (desired state) increases, so does awareness of the gap between the dream and present state.

We also drop our dreams and ideas when we forget our connection to them. Our most urgent needs, activities and problems make goals dim and weaken. We simply stop asking ourselves, "What do I (we) really want to create?"

Of course, such a danger is more threatening for our long-term goals. Our deepest and most distant dreams, either personal or group dreams, frequently die because we forget our connection to them.

So, we have here two preoccupations: to maintain alive our long-term dreams (our vision) and to keep our outcome ("idea") clear in any daily situation.

The method of asking questions is helpful in both cases. But we need to develop a kind of habit. As soon as we wake up we can ask some essential questions. One of them could be related to our highest and most cherished dream. For example, we may ask ourselves:

— What's my highest dream in life?
— What's my purpose? What am I alive for?
— What's the most important thing for me?

If we start our day having in mind our dream or purpose in life, we will experience its benefits during our daily journey. Suppose, for example, that you are getting involved in a useless argument. At that very moment your inner artist will remind you that such an argument is not your dream. You have something much more important than your point of view about, let us say, a movie, a politician, a piece of art.

Try a very short exercise. Visualise yourself in the middle of a problem, conflict, inconvenience. Get in there. Feel the tension. Interrupt this negative feeling by asking yourself:

— What's really important in my life?

If you have a heartfelt, honest answer like, "The most important thing for me is peace, internal and external peace," you will probably drop the passionate defence of your point of view. I cannot tell you what the results of this exercise will be for you. Try by yourself.

My experience shows me that this kind of awareness about my purpose or most distant dream helps me to diminish the momentousness of many things which are not important at all.

The other value of keeping your goal in mind is effectiveness. If you know what you really want, it will be easier to persevere on the track that takes you to the fulfillment of your dream. This is basic in great people. In fact, it was Einstein who recommended to keep our goal firm and to change the ways to achieve it.

A second aspect of keeping our goal in mind is related with our different activities throughout our daily journey. You can keep your objective clear in any situation. Suppose you want to express your love to your daughter, but a misunderstanding appears during the conversation. You blame her and she blames you. She is getting angry and you too. Suddenly you recall your own goal: "I want to let her know that I appreciate and love her." As soon as this thought flashes in your mind, you stop the argument you have fallen into.

To be specific, try now. Ask yourself, "What's my objective while reading this page?" Once you have the answer, keep the same objective clear during the time you continue reading this book.

When you stop reading and start a new activity, ask yourself, "What's my objective?" Having an answer keeps your objective clear during that activity.

5. FLEXIBILITY

I suppose that it is difficult to be creative without being flexible. It is true that some masterpieces are the fruit of just one trial. But these are exceptions. Most fruits of human creativity have required lots of trials and, therefore, effort and time.

I like to repeat the example of Thomas Alva Edison. After he had tried unsuccessfully 1,999 times to perfect the electric bulb, one of his colleagues asked him, "Will the next be your 2,000th failure?" He answered, "Not failure. Just the discovery of another way not to invent the electric bulb."

Notice that he is following the four steps of the T.O.T.E. that I mentioned in the last section:

1- He has a clear idea of his GOAL: the electric bulb.
2- He has taken action: 2,000 trials.
3- He uses his SENSORY ACUITY: he has discovered another way not to invent the electric bulb.
4- He deploys his FLEXIBILITY: is ready to try thousands of times. He keeps changing the means.

Without such flexibility he would not be the inventor of the electric bulb. In the same way, you will not fulfil your dreams and ideas without being flexible.

Today, think about those goals you have been trying to attain along just one path. Afterwards, change and use one or more different ways to reach your goal. Perhaps you have scolded your son because he got poor results at school. Try a different way to motivate him. Promise him a reward if he improves. Help him associate study with his favorite sport. Help him to link pleasure to studying. And so on. Be flexible.

With your group or by yourself try the following exercise. Of course, you can repeat it during your spare time. For example, do it while you are taking your shower.

1- Take a comfortable body posture. Breathe deeply several times. Search for the best and for the most beautiful aspect of your present reality. Use your *Circle of Excellence* or the anchor you have to trigger a resourceful state.

2- Call to mind one of your goals or even your most distant dream in life. Think of the *action* you are going to take to achieve it. By the way, imagine the criterion you will use as evidence procedure, so that you may employ your *sensory acuity* to realise whether you are getting closer to your goal.

3- Now imagine that you take action. But you apply your *sensory acuity* and realise that such a means or path does not take you to your goal. What are you going to do?

Visualise a change. Use a different way to reach your goal. But this one does not work either. Imagine another way. Neither this one nor the next activity work. Keep changing. Train your mind to be more flexible.

4- After ten, twenty, or more trials, remember Thomas Alva Edison who made thousands of trials to invent the electric bulb. Be ready, like him, to keep changing until you get the results you really want.

5- Share this experience with another person or with your group. Tell them what ways you will use to find out more and more alternatives to attain your goals.

On the other hand, do not forget that life is flexible. A plant in your house moves its branches and leaves towards the window in search of light. The Monarch butterflies fly about six thousand kilometers from Canada to Mexico each year. They are flexible enough to move to a country where the winter is mild.

Creativity is just an expression of life. Therefore, you are expected to be as flexible as life. In this way, your inner artist will be able to express his creativity.

6. TIMING

When you take action to attain your goals or your dreams, you should consider time as a variable of your creativity.

Sometimes, creativity flies on the winds of time dressed as opportunity. If you do not take it, you will lose it. Thus, you, your group and other people need to seize the moment and make the most of opportunities.

Very often, you may be too impatient to finish what you start. But if a particular activity you have undertaken requires more time, you need to give it more time.

The opposite may happen too. Certain activities should be finished as soon as possible. Otherwise, you will lack motivation and perseverance. You will probably quit the creative process when you are halfway to your goal.

You probably start to suspect that time plays an important role within the T.O.T.E. Let us take an example. Imagine your *goal* is to have warm water in the shower. It will be more difficult to attain it if there is a ten-second delay before the water temperature adjusts, than when the delay takes only one or two seconds.

In fact, suppose you make your first *test*. You realise that the water is cold. You *operate* by adjusting the hot water faucet. You apply several *tests*. After ten seconds the water remains cold. There is no response to your action. You perceive that your act has had no effect. You react by continuing to turn up the hot water.

One more *test* shows you that the hot water arrives, but 190-degree water spurts from the shower. You jump out and turn it back. After another delay, it is cold again. A sequence of *tests* make you *operate* again and again taking more time in the balancing loop process.

There is a lesson here. The more aggressive you are in your behaviour—the more drastically you turn the knobs—the longer it will take you to have warm water. Your impatient behaviour produces exactly the opposite of what you really want. It produces instability and oscillation, instead of taking you to your goal.

We need, therefore, to consider time as an important variable within a system. Time affects your action. Sometimes you need to be as fast and effective as possible. Sometimes you need to be patient and to take your time. Let us do today's exercise.

1- Have a comfortable body position. Breathe deeply. Discover what is beautiful and what is very good in your present environment. Use your anchor and trigger a resourceful state.

2- Consider the action you have taken or you are going to take to reach one of your goals. Find out how time can affect your action. Does the goal demand quick action or does it require time and patience? Does your goal require a little of both strategies? What other interferences of time are possible?

3- Use the mindmapping technique to learn more about time as a variable in your action which, in one way or another, is a part of a T.O.T.E.

4- Share your mind map or your list of possible interferences of time in your action.

7. INVENTING

Certainly, each of us is an inventor. We invent lies, gossip, dramas, and we also create ideas, solutions, plans, desires, goals, dreams, and so on. Our inner artist is always ready to serve us. We can profit by his creativity either to destroy or to build.

You normally invent when you act under the creative urge of your inner artist. But you can do so with more awareness and efficiency. Let me suggest some exercises for today.

Do what you normally do in your daily routine a little differently. Brush your teeth in a different way. Change your way of eating: start with fruit, do not add salt to any food, avoid what is fried, identify the specific taste of each food, chew slowly, and so on. Do other habitual things in a new manner.

Take the following objects and use them in a completely new way:

— Pencil
— Paper
— Book
— Fruit
— Knife
— Glass
— Key
— Chair
— TV
— Blanket

Plan some trips you never before dreamed of. Specify the details of a trip to Europe, Asia, Africa, America, Australia. Who is coming with you? How are you going to travel? When exactly? How long?

Invent a story or even a parable like those Jesus created to deliver his message of peace, joy and love. If you decide to imagine that story in your group, do it with the intention of publishing it.

Suppose that you, and your companions if you are working in a group, have infinite power to change humankind. Invent a story about the changes you would introduce in this world to make it more human and happier. What kind of interrelations would you introduce in our society? What economic, political and social changes would you make? Which moral and spiritual values would you develop? And so forth.

Imagine that God offers you the opportunity to live three other lives. What kind of person would you choose to be? What would your beliefs be as that person? What capabilities and skills would you have? What would you do in each of those lives? Where and when would you like to live those three lives?

Suppose that you, or each of you, are ready to become an inventor in your own area of expertise. Go through the following process:

1- Breathe deeply. Enjoy the best and the most beautiful thing present in your environment. Have a resourceful state.

2- According to your talents, ask yourself, "What can I do for others?"

3- Take a further step, and ask yourself, "What can I create to improve the quality of others' lives?"

4- Continue with the following questions, "Why do I want to create that for them?" "Why is it important that I create that?"

5- Ask yourself, "Who am I or who will I become if I take action today and produce that (product, service, prayer, idea)?"

If possible, start right now. Take action immediately. Invent. Enrich this world with your talents. Add value to people's lives. Be the artist you really are. Please the Creator who endowed you with so many talents.

110

V- RESOURCES OF THE INNER CRITIC

You might deploy your inner critic to say that it is too late to introduce the critic in this creative process. You might explain that the inner critic should intervene after the creation of new ideas.

You are right. I agree with you. Our inner critic should express his opinion immediately after the production of new ideas.

I held back his intervention until now because he must learn to use his resources on behalf of our creativity and never against it.

The reality is that our inner critic interferes too much with our creative process. Even more, he prevents most of us from being creative. For this reason I decided to put him aside in the hope that you do the same. Of course, he has very valuable resources which we need in the creative process. It is better, however, to listen to his voice when your creative activity is well developed.

The inner critic, as you can imagine, is connected with the left side of the brain. And just like that side, he is verbal, logic, analytic. He repeats the lessons given by adults when we were children. Sometimes he is like an unbearable judge who is ever ready to criticise, condemn and torture.

According to my experience, we need to be very, very careful and protect ourselves from the snares of our inner critic. After that, we must face his arrogance and his cunning. Once we learn to protect ourselves, we are able to transform him into a friend. Then he will help us improve our creativity.

1. THE CRITIC WITHIN

The inner critic, of course, is well-intentioned. He wants to spare us shame and pain. He represents those adults who, during our childhood, tried to teach us how to look good and to behave appropriately in order to succeed in the world. Most of all, they wanted us to be safe and sound, successful and happy.

"The Inner Critic is remarkable in a number of different ways. It seems to operate with heightened awareness in all areas. It can see, hear and feel what is wrong with us as though it had the most advanced technology at its disposal. It has the intelligence of a genius, an uncanny intuition, an ability to analyse our feelings and motivations, a sweeping gaze that notices the tiniest of details, and, in general, an unerring ability to see and to magnify all our faults and shortcomings. It seems to be a lot more intelligent and perceptive than we ordinary mortals are."[1]

He expresses himself, within our minds, through short, powerful and convincing sentences like:

— You have no talent.
— You don't have good ideas.
— You cannot do so much.
— You will do a bad job.
— You will look like a fool.
— You won't finish.
— You need more inspiration.
— You aren't a genius.
— You don't deserve such success.
— It's too late. If you haven't become a fully functioning artist yet, you won't ever.
— You're getting old.
— You won't make it, unless you work twice as hard as everyone else.

[1] H.Stone & S.Stone, *Embracing Your Inner Critic*. New York, NY: HarperSanFrancisco, 1993, p. 9.

Strangely enough, our inner critic has a good intention when he utters this kind of statements. He wants us to be okay. He really wants us to make it in the world, to have a good job, to be creative, to be successful. But he does not know the limits of his role. He does not know when enough is enough. He even grows until he is out of control and begins to undermine us and to do real damage.

We need, therefore, to become aware of his excess and destructiveness. Certainly, we need more than simple awareness of the snares of our inner critic. We may be trapped by his cunning statements in spite of our awareness. Nevertheless, when we know his subtleties we are able to protect ourselves and to nourish our inner artist.

There are different ways to recognise your inner critic. One of them is to pay more attention to your thoughts. As soon as you realise any self-criticism, jot down that statement on a piece of paper. If you think, for example, "I cannot be creative," write this sentence down. Through this simple action you will unmask your inner critic.

I am presupposing here that those statements of our inner critic are made unconsciously. We are rather unaware we think them. That is why we need to become aware of them.

We can use the mindmapping technique to detect our inner critic's negative statements faster. I offer you a diagram for that purpose. Within the central circle write one of your dreams, desires or ideas. Around the centre write down your doubts, negative beliefs and criticism starting each sentence with *but...*

Certainly, it is much better if you employ images or graphic representations of your dreams, goals or ideas.

I will offer you an example. On the next page you will have a space to do today's exercise. It will help to identify some of the negative beliefs of your inner critic.

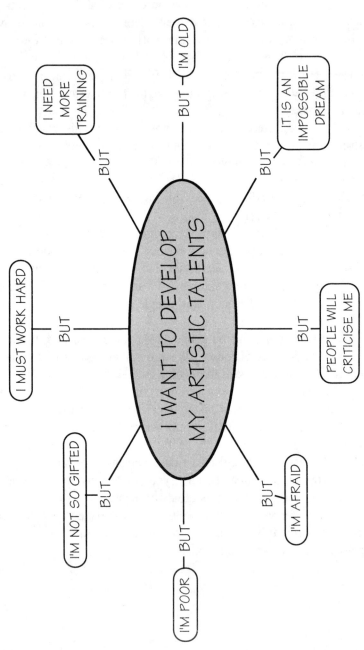

114

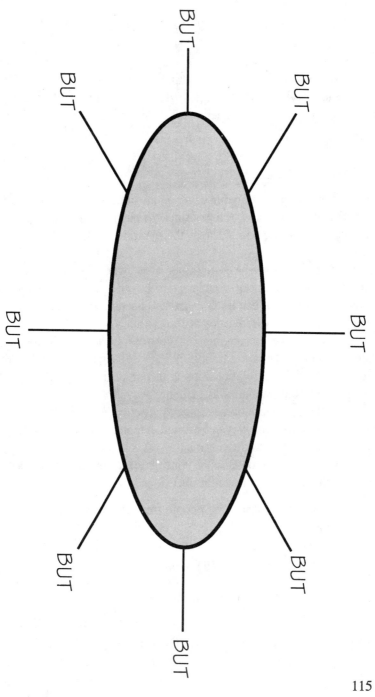

115

2. NEGOTIATING WITH THE CRITIC

The critic is yourself. You are a unity or an organic system. You are the same with different roles: daughter, wife, mother, sister, psychologist, housewife, friend and also:

> dreamer,
> realist,
> **critic.**

Very frequently, your critic is an oppressor and the realist and the dreamer are the victims. You can imagine that a revolution is needed to destroy the tyrannical oppression of the critic.

This is partly true. Our inner artist who is both a dreamer and a realist, requires freedom to be the one he really is. Simultaneously, the inner artist needs the perspective, enlightenment and discoveries of the critic.

In brief, we cannot think of destroying the inner critic. His role is important in creativity. What we should dream is the creation of win-win relationships with our critic. Neither his way nor our way, but another way, a better way.

Through negotiation we search for that *better way* and for many other excellent ways. Through negotiation we all win: the dreamer, the realist and the critic.

You can negotiate with your inner critic using the same steps as in any normal negotiation:

People: Separate the people from the problem.
Intention: Focus on people's intentions not positions.
Options: Generate a variety of alternatives and possibilities before deciding what to do.
Criteria: Insist that the result of negotiation be based on some objective standard.

With respect to the first point, *separate people from the problem,* you already know that the critic is one thing, and the problem of his tyrannical oppression is another thing. Once you have this distinction clear, you may proceed to the second step.

I previously underlined the good intention that drives our inner critic to the excess of becoming very demanding. He is an oppressor because he wants you to be loved, to be successful, to be healthy.

Thus, agreement between your inner artist and your inner critic is possible because they agree at the level of intention. Both of them want the best for you.

The third step is an exercise for the inner artist. Alternatives that satisfy both the critic's demands and the artist's desires must be found. For example, if your inner critic makes you think that you must work too hard to develop you artistic talents, find alternatives that satisfy the critic's concern and you own desire:

— I can follow an art course instead of playing cards with my friends twice a week.
— I can draw and paint instead of watching TV.
— I can draw something while travelling on the Underground.
— I can draw with my grandchildren instead of going to the park.
— I can draw and paint instead of reading the newspaper for so long.
— I can read more books on art than on other topics.
— I can stop drinking on Saturday night and meet friends with artistic interests.
— I can visit one of the best painters in the city and take him as my model. In this way I can improve more quickly.
— I can draw with my grandchildren in the park and even in the street.
— I can watch the movies from an artistic perspective.
— I can, I can, I can...

Alternatives of this kind might satisfy the requirements of your inner critic and give up the opportunity to transform your ideas into deeds.

The fourth step for negotiating is an invitation to use objective criteria when you arrive at an agreement with your inner critic. Perhaps it is not healthy to stop going to the park with your grandchildren. Perhaps the artist you intend to take for your model has a style which is incompatible with your personality. And so on.

You may negotiate with your inner critic in another way. John Grinder and Judith DeLozier taught me the following procedure:

1- *Agree about the disagreement.* Ask your inner critic, "Do we agree that you think *I'm too old* and I think *I can manage in spite of my age?*"

2- *Clarify the intentions.* Tell your inner critic, "I know your intention is to assure that I keep healthy, happy, and loved by others. And my intention is almost the same; I want to have something good that will keep me active after my retirement. If I do not have anything to do, I'll get sad, depressed and sick, like many others."

3- *Generate win-win alternatives.* You have the above example.

4- *Specify the agreement.* Choose among the alternatives the one which is mutually beneficial and satisfying. Next decide how to achieve it.

5- *Conclusion.* Express your feelings of gratitude. Open the door for further negotiations.

NLP has another way to *negotiate between parts* of the same self. This time, *part X* corresponds to your inner artist, and *part Y* to your inner critic.

1- Ask the part that is being interrupted—part X—the following questions:

A- What is your positive intention?
B- Which part(s) is (are) interrupting you?—part Y—

2- Ask the same questions to part Y:

A- What is your positive intention?

B- Does X ever interfere with your achieving your intention?

3- If both parts interrupt each other at times, you are now ready to negotiate an agreement. (If not, this model is not appropriate, so switch to another reframing model. If Y interferes with X, but X does not interfere with Y, try the above exercise or Six-Step Reframing for Y).

A- Ask Y if its intention is important enough that it would be willing to not interrupt X so that it could receive the same treatment in return.

B- Ask X whether it would be willing to not interrupt Y, if it were not interrupted by Y.

4- Ask each part if it will actually agree to do the above for a specified amount of time. If either part becomes dissatisfied for any reason, it is to signal the person that there is a need to renegotiate.

5- Ecological check: "Are any other parts involved in this?" "Are there any other parts that interrupt this part, or that utilise these interruptions?" If so, renegotiate.

3. CHANGING NEGATIVE BELIEFS

Your inner critic is powerful because he is part of yourself. He speaks from within. So, it is natural for you to believe in him. In consequence, most of his statements are beliefs. You actually believe that you are too old, that you are not a gifted person, that you do not have enough money, and so on.

What you believe, either true or false, becomes real to you. Think of the so-called "placebo." It is just a starch pill but it may cure you if you believe it is the best medicine on the market.

NLP has great news regarding our beliefs: we can change them if we want to. We are able to get rid of the disempowering ones. Simultaneously, we have the necessary resources to install empowering beliefs.

In fact, our beliefs are powerful enough to hold back our capabilities or to release them. In other words, our creative talents are controlled by our beliefs. If you believe you can't, you cannot. If you believe you can, you can. Of course, I am talking about normal and reasonable things.

The specific question now is how to substitute our disempowering beliefs, that is, how do we install new and empowering beliefs instead of the disempowering ones?

One way is to associate pain with a negative belief and pleasure with a positive one. Keep asking yourself from morning till night:

— What is good in this new belief?
— What are the benefits of this empowering belief?
— What pleasure can I derive from this positive belief?

On the other hand, ask yourself sincerely:

— What's bad in this negative belief?
— What are the consequences of my disempowering belief?
— What pain is this negative belief causing me?

Certainly, it is important that you get answers you feel in your body and even in your gut. If you do, you will experience an effective change of beliefs.

Another exercise implies several resources: submodalities, kinesthetic associations and emotional state.

1- Take a comfortable body position. Breathe deeply. Awaken your state of hope. Trust in God and/or in your natural resources. Take for granted that you will succeed in changing your beliefs.

2- Find a symbol for your negative belief. Let us say it is like a balloon. Give it all the visual characteristics or submodalities of your negative belief: size, colour, distance, brightness, etc.

3- Put your negative belief on your left side, perhaps on your left leg if you are sitting. Leave it there.

4- Now remember a time when you started to doubt something that you used to believe with all your heart. Revive the body sensations of doubting. Make them more intense.

5- Collect all these sensations and feelings of doubt with your left hand. Pour the sensations of doubt over the balloon. Observe how the symbol of the negative belief changes. See the change of brightness, colour, distance, size... Perhaps the balloon shrinks. Maybe it grows bigger and bigger until it explodes...

6- Now imagine a symbol for the empowering belief you want to have. Let us say it is another balloon, but with other visual characteristics in brightness, colour, size, distance, etc. At the beginning this new belief may seem too dim, pale, small, distant, etc. Put it on your right leg.

7- Remember something you believe in without a scrap of doubt, something you believe with all your heart. Observe its visual submodalities. Keep them in mind, since you are going to infuse them into the new belief.

8- Keep in your mind and heart the same belief you evoked in the last step. Observe this time the body sensations and feelings it produces in you. Pay attention to its kinesthetic submodalities: area of your body, intensity, texture, temperature, duration, weight.

9- Collect all the sensations and feelings of your strong belief with your right hand. Pour these sensations into your new belief. See the change of size, colour, brightness, distance, clarity in your new belief.

10- Take the new belief and introduce it into your heart. See and feel the empowering belief within your heart.

11- Take the old negative belief or the rest of it and keep it in that drawer of your memory where you have what you used to believe.

12- See and feel the new belief in your heart. Breathe deeply. Move your body. Feel the satisfaction and joy of having accomplished an important change in your heart.

13- Share this experience with somebody else.

4. CRITERIA TO SELECT YOUR IDEAS

The change of beliefs is an essential part of the process of transforming your inner critic into your friend and associate. Sometimes you will struggle with him to prevent him imposing his negative view on your inner artist. Sometimes you will offer him just a passive resistance, and act as if you had not heard him. Sometimes you will talk to him in a friendly way. Sometimes you will negotiate with him, finding win-win solutions. Sometimes he will be a real friend to you.

Suppose that you have already gone through this process. Your inner critic is a real friend who shares his talents with you. In this case, you are in the better position to select your ideas or to choose from several alternatives.

You are the one who will state his own criteria. And I take for granted that you may establish your personal criteria on one hand, and objective criteria on the other hand.

Write your personal criteria and what you consider objective criteria within the big circle in the centre of the following diagram. In the small circles write down the ideas that are closest to those criteria.

GOAL: SOCIAL CREATIVITY

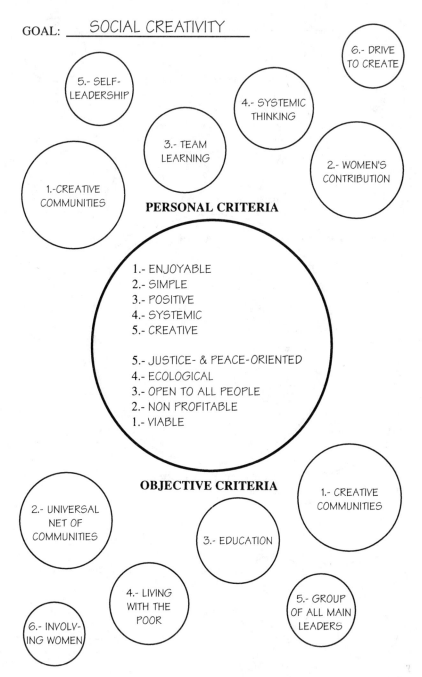

5.- SELF-LEADERSHIP

6.- DRIVE TO CREATE

4.- SYSTEMIC THINKING

3.- TEAM LEARNING

2.- WOMEN'S CONTRIBUTION

1.-CREATIVE COMMUNITIES

PERSONAL CRITERIA

1.- ENJOYABLE
2.- SIMPLE
3.- POSITIVE
4.- SYSTEMIC
5.- CREATIVE

5.- JUSTICE- & PEACE-ORIENTED
4.- ECOLOGICAL
3.- OPEN TO ALL PEOPLE
2.- NON PROFITABLE
1.- VIABLE

OBJECTIVE CRITERIA

1.- CREATIVE COMMUNITIES

2.- UNIVERSAL NET OF COMMUNITIES

3.- EDUCATION

4.- LIVING WITH THE POOR

5.- GROUP OF ALL MAIN LEADERS

6.- INVOLVING WOMEN

GOAL: _____

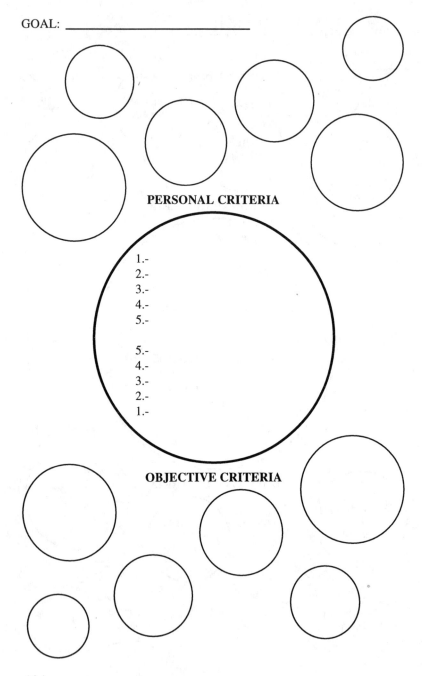

PERSONAL CRITERIA

1.-
2.-
3.-
4.-
5.-

5.-
4.-
3.-
2.-
1.-

OBJECTIVE CRITERIA

5. SELECTION OF IDEAS

The last exercise presupposes that each goal demands its own criteria. You cannot keep the same criteria for all possible goals. Some products require more beauty than others. Some others involve a diminishing size, like personal computers. And so on.

Once you have your personal and objective criteria for a specific goal, use the last diagram to classify your ideas as to the alternative ways to achieve that goal. Afterwards, you should choose. Of course, the idea which meets more of your personal criteria and more objective criteria should be the chosen one.

When you employ a diagram like the last one or simply a mind map, you involve both brains in the selection of one idea. Simultaneously, it leaves a space for other alternatives. Remember that lateral thinking goes beyond the goal of having "the best idea."

On the other hand, the election of just one idea might be difficult sometimes. Remember, however, that your unconscious mind plays an important role in the process of decision making.

Each person has a specific strategy for making a decision. But most of us, especially artists, arrive at the *decision point* through a kinesthetic experience, i.e. body sensation and feeling.

NLP offers the following example:

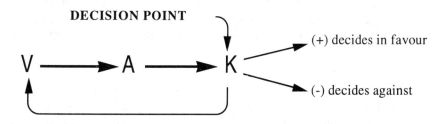

Here the individual makes a decision by looking at possibilities (**V**), describing them to himself (**A**) and then deriving body sensations and feelings (**K**) on the basis of those descriptions. The internal feelings constitute the decision point in this particular strategy. If the feelings are congruently positive (+), the person decides in favour of that particular idea; if the feelings are congruently negative (-), the person decides against it. If the feelings are ambivalent or incongruent (?), the individual operates by looking back at the options and by describing them again.

Depending, then, on the goal or outcome you are working toward, you will want to emphasise different kinds of content representations at this step. If it is appropriate for you to incline the inner critic (or person) in favour, you will emphasise a positive kinesthetic representation (+). If you are better off deciding against, you will emphasise negative kinesthetic sensations (-). If you want many alternatives to be considered, then stress ambiguity in your (his) feelings (?).

If you want to do the last exercise, draw an arrow to connect the criteria with the idea that meets them. Have a look at the example about social creativity. It seems that creation of "creative communities" meets all the criteria suggested both as personal and objective.

After that, go through a decision strategy like the one above: look at possibilities, describe them for yourself (or for your inner critic), observe your body sensations and feelings about that idea.

Share your decision with somebody else, if you are making this creative journey by yourself. If it is a group experience, find out the group preferences. If necessary, negotiate an agreement on the best idea.

It is important, from the systemic point of view, to keep our mind open to other alternatives and possibilities. We know that a lateral-thinking perspective opens a horizon beyond the best idea. There are further possibilities to get other much better ideas than the one we consider the best. For the moment, this is the best available to our perception. But reality is pregnant with many other wonderful ideas.

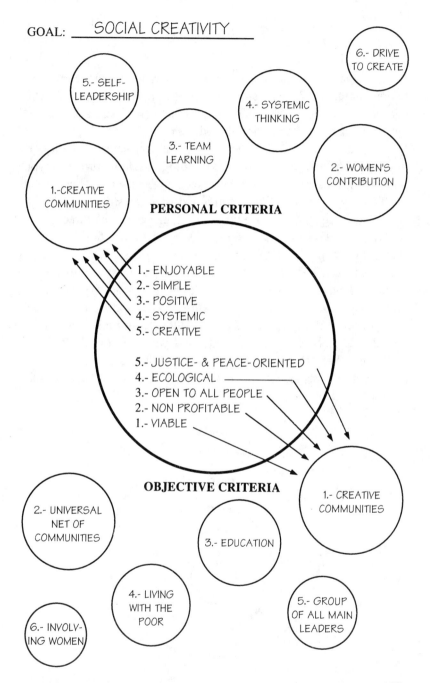

GOAL: SOCIAL CREATIVITY

6.- DRIVE TO CREATE

5.- SELF-LEADERSHIP

4.- SYSTEMIC THINKING

3.- TEAM LEARNING

2.- WOMEN'S CONTRIBUTION

1.-CREATIVE COMMUNITIES

PERSONAL CRITERIA

1.- ENJOYABLE
2.- SIMPLE
3.- POSITIVE
4.- SYSTEMIC
5.- CREATIVE

5.- JUSTICE- & PEACE-ORIENTED
4.- ECOLOGICAL
3.- OPEN TO ALL PEOPLE
2.- NON PROFITABLE
1.- VIABLE

OBJECTIVE CRITERIA

1.- CREATIVE COMMUNITIES

2.- UNIVERSAL NET OF COMMUNITIES

3.- EDUCATION

4.- LIVING WITH THE POOR

5.- GROUP OF ALL MAIN LEADERS

6.- INVOLV-ING WOMEN

6. THE BIG PICTURE

If you have a big picture of a reality—person, group, company, nation, humankind, planet—try to fit your ideas into it. You will certainly discover which ideas fit in better, which ones don't, which other ones are required by whole reality.

In other words, use the big picture you have of reality. If you are a believer, you are lucky. Religious faith provides you with a big picture. And this helps you to be a critic, because it enables you to realise what fits in it and what doesn't.

The big picture provided by faith contains three basic realities: GOD-WORLD-PEOPLE. What's more, faith offers a specific concept about these three main realities. "God is love." He loves each person without limits. So, God says: "love each other as I have loved you." And our world is an expression of God's love for each of us. Therefore, "God took the man and settled him in the garden of Eden to cultivate and take care of it" (Gn 2:15). According to this text, God wants us to take care of our planet. We are not supposed to contaminate and destroy it.

Let me represent the big picture of faith with a simple diagram:

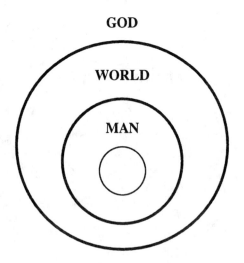

There is a line which connects God with people passing through the world: LIFE. God is the Creator of life. He has given us the treasure of life. With life He has endowed us with His creative power, since we are able to create life and to improve its quality and value.

From this perspective, we may evaluate our ideas and find the best. Simultaneously, we may remain open to further ideas which might be better than today's best.

Some questions help us select our best ideas within the context of our big picture. Of course, I respect your faith or religious beliefs. If you are not a believer, just widen your picture as much as possible.

— Does my (our) best idea fit in the harmony of this whole reality?
— Does my (our) idea or goal respect and enhance life?
— Does my (our) best idea benefit humankind?
— Does my (our) best idea match the order and evolution of our world?
— Does my (our) idea or goal support God's plan of love and life?
— Does my (our) best idea achieve God's loving will?

Certainly, you have other kinds of big pictures. For instance, you could design a time line that starts with the Big Bang, passes through our present time and ends somewhere as yet unknown.

BIG BANG   PRESENT   BIG CRUNCH ?   ETERNITY

— Does my (our) best idea fit in the creative evolution of the world?
— Does my (our) idea enhance an increasing quality of our universe?

129

— Does my (our) idea enhance life and awareness within the cosmos?
— Does my (our) idea support the progress of human history?
— Does my (our) idea improve human life and environmental ecology?

7. THE CRITIC'S DISCOVERIES

You have probably realised that the process of classifying and selecting your ideas yields different kinds of discoveries. In fact, this is one of the essential tasks of the critic: the generation of discoveries.

While you examine your idea within the context of the whole, you may discover certain aspects that you have not taken into consideration. Many important discoveries are just a fruit of an unconscious incubation process. Sometimes, they appear during the hard work of study and research. And many times they are a specific contribution of the inner critic.

At this point I presuppose a positive attitude in our inner critic. In consequence, I think that our critic's contribution consists of statements that generate feelings of insatisfaction and doubt. Perhaps something like "the earth can't be the centre of the universe." "The earth must be round." "There must be a cure for cancer." "This idea could be expressed in a more beautiful way." And so on.

The method of asking questions opens the perspective of further discoveries:

— What is my purpose in life? Why am I alive?
— How can I achieve my purpose?
— What could I contribute to enhance the value of people's life?
— What could bring a stable peace among peoples?
— What could generate a new economic order in our world?

— What could be a new way of painting?
— What kind of cities will be thoroughly human?
— What is the best way to keep ourselves happy and healthy?
— What's the way to guarantee constant and never-ending improvement?
— What do we need to avoid any kind of violence and evil?
— How can we create the world we all need and desire?

Questions like these presuppose that you are going to make more than one discovery. And in all these questions there is an intervention of our inner critic. He provokes unpleasant feelings with respect to our *present state*. He pushes us to discover both our *desired state* (dreams, ideas, goals) and the necessary *resources*.

When you criticise, mostly when your inner critic is empowering, you enter the path of discoveries. Sooner or later you will discover something new, useful and viable. On the other hand, the exploratory road is the normal one to lead us to discoveries. Try a short exercise.

1- Take one of your dreams or ideas. Perhaps the idea which you consider the best. Maybe a product or service you want to implement.

2- Use second position to find out the response of people who will thrive on that idea. Step into the shoes of people as different as possible.

3- From these people's perspective, a) explore and b) criticise the idea selected as the best.

4- Jot down a list of observations coming from different people's exploration of your idea.

6- Compare the different critiques coming from different people.

7- Take the most useful observations and critiques. Compare them.

8- Choose the most useful and viable ideas. Ply them to your idea.

9- Modify and perfect your idea. Describe it in practical—operational—terms. Have it ready to be implemented.

In today's creative practice or that of any other day of this week, check the *formation standards* NLP offers you to evaluate your ideas. Robert Dilts and Todd Epstein apply them to creativity as shown:

Dreamer

1- The goal is stated in positive terms. That is, it states what you do want as opposed to what you don't want.

Questions: What do you want? What is possible? What is the payoff?

Realist

2- The goal can be initiated and maintained by the person or group desiring it.

Question: What specifically will **you** do to achieve this goal?

3- The goal is testable in sensory experience.

Question: How, specifically, will you know when you achieve your goal?

Critic

4- The goal preserves the positive by-products of the current behaviour or activity.

Questions: What positive things do you get out of your present way of doing things? How will you maintain those things in your new goal?

5- The goal is appropriately contextualised and ecologically sound.

Questions: Under what conditions would you not want to implement this new goal? Who and what else could it affect?

The last exercise for today is quite simple. Adopt the physiology that Robert Dilts has detected in people who are playing the role of the critic:

"Eyes down. Head down and tilted. Posture angular."

VI- SOCIAL CREATIVITY

I decided to include this chapter because I know people in America, Europe and Africa who want to do something for other people. NLP trainers, for example, dream of *creating a world to which people want to belong*. Most of all, you and I are human beings. We realise, one way or another, that we all need and deserve a better world.

A deep desire beats in the hearts of many people who want to create that *world to which people want to belong*. The deployment of our social creativity is one way to create a better world.

In fact, Jesus of Nazareth employed his social and spiritual creativity to picture that world to which people want to belong. Jesus' dreams are current and alive. We need a world of justice, forgiveness, peace, love, hope, joy, health, faith and happiness like the one Jesus has depicted and initiated.

In this chapter, i.e. in this sixth week of our creative journey, I will follow Jesus' footsteps as much as possible. He started his great revolution of love through a social or interpersonal process. Of course, he opened the spiritual perspective as well. He set God as the centre and goal of his social creativity. That is why the next chapter is devoted to spiritual creativity.

Once again I repeat that you deserve all my respect, regardless of whether you are a Christian, religious believer, or non-believer. I mention Jesus, however, as a leader who dreamed of that world to which people want to belong. He worked for the creation of that world. He offered his own life to start the creation of such a world. He continues supporting his followers bent on creating a world to which people want to belong.

1. SUFFERING WITH PEOPLE

In the first chapter, or during the first week, I recommended feeling people's needs in order to awaken our inner artist. The inner artist is very sensitive. In normal conditions, he is able to sympathise with people's needs and suffering. So, if we expose our inner artist to get in touch with poor, sick and needy people, he will react in a creative way. He will dream of creating a better world for all people without any exceptions.

Today, in this section, we will take a further step in relationship with suffering people. I offer you a list of different possibilities to get in touch with people in need. Of course, you and I are one of those people. We also have needs, troubles and grievances. But, let me concentrate on those who are probably in worse conditions than ours.

If you belong to an organisation, perhaps to a multinational company, discover the value of this chapter for the future of your group.[1] What happens in nature or to humankind will sooner or later affect your own company. Therefore, it is good for every human being and group to create a world to which people want to belong.

Today's exercise has a specific goal: to keep our inner artist awake and creative. I believe, like Yoshiro NakaMats, that our best and most creative achievements come from responding to people's needs. Therefore, I invite you to explore and discover your own way of keeping in touch with people's implicit or explicit expectations.

1- In your dreamer's body position—head and eyes up, posture symmetrical and relaxed—trigger your resourceful state.

---

[1] Cf. P.Senge, *The Fifth Discipline*. New York, NY: Doubleday, 1990. A.Robbins, *Awaken the Giant Within*. New York, NY: Simon & Schuster, 1991. M.Scott Peck, *A World Waiting to Be Born*. New York, NY: Bantam, 1993.

2- Remember a time when you felt deeply moved by people's suffering and, therefore, willing to do something for them. Let us say that you experienced a state of creative compassion.

See again what you were seeing at that moment. Listen to the voice and sounds you were listening to. Feel in your body the feelings of compassion and readiness to do something. Intensify these sensations and feelings of creative compassion.

3- Associate this state of creative compassion with an anchor—a red circle one step to your right, a specific sign in your right hand, an image or music in your head, etc.

4- Remember another situation which gave you the opportunity to experience that creative compassion. Repeat the above procedure.

5- Search for two or three other similar experiences and anchor them.

Once you have created this new anchor, take a rest for a minute or two. Then proceed to the second exercise.

1- Use your anchor for creative compassion first. Once you have elicited such a state, use your anchor to trigger a resourceful state. Be sure that you are in your dreamer's body posture.

2- Visualise the dreams that your creative compassion suggests to you. Be free. Produce all kinds of dreams that are beneficial for people. Prefer, however, those dreams that belong to your area of expertise.

3- Choose the simplest and most viable dream related with social change and improvement. Of course, such a dream should also be connected with the bigger dream of creating a world to which people want to belong.

4- Transform your dream into a movie. Visualise or narrate that film for yourself first. Later on, share the movie of your social dream with another person. Hopefully you are doing the exercise within a group. In this case the sharing is in pairs first. Next you share in groups of four people. Then you sort out the common patterns in your dreams and share these patterns with the whole group.

5- Close the exercise with an act of hope. Think that most social changes had a beginning as simple as this exercise. Trust in God or in life to nourish your hope. Feel certain that you will contribute, at least with your optimism, to creating a world to which people want to belong.

Finally, consider with somebody else or with your group, the following possibilities of commitment to people:

1- Living with the poorest like Jesus, Gandhi, Mother Teresa, and many other promoters of social changes.

2- Working, in any way, for the poor and needy.

3- Visiting poor, sick, oppressed, suffering people.

4- Keeping in touch with them through social media—TV, radio, press—and being committed to them through a life of simplicity, honesty, love and generosity at home and at the workplace.

5- Being committed to them through a constant and never-ending improvement in love, justice and peace. This improvement will be lived by relatives, friends, colleagues, and society.

6- Being committed to them through prayer, sacrifice and self-donation to God for the sake of all humankind.

Of course, you invent your own way to be committed to people. Your commitment to others will awaken your inner artist. Not only that, your inner artist will reach the fullness of his creativity, driven by the creative force of love.

2. PARTNERS IN SOCIAL COMMITMENT

You need partners if you want to cooperate in creating a world to which people want to belong. You alone can do a lot for others.

But you will do much more if you form a team with people who want to be creators of a better world.

Your task for today is quite specific. You are going to use the process of exploration-discovery to sort out some individuals who could be your companions in this adventure. Remember, there are no perfect human beings. We are imperfect. Even the saints had their own imperfections or, at least, their own human limitations. Only God is perfect. Therefore, do not expect to find super heroes who will always be polite, generous, joyful, sincere and sinless. No. Not at all.

Jesus chose ordinary people. Peter, the one he chose as the rock of his Church, betrayed him. So, be ready to imitate Jesus. Accept in your group even a Judas who might betray you even unto death. In order to spread the Church, "God chose those who by human standards are fools to shame the wise; he chose those who by human standards are weak to shame the strong, those who by human standards are common and contemptible—indeed those who count for nothing—to reduce to nothing all those that do count for something, so that no human being might feel boastful before God" (1 Co 1:27-29).

In brief, I would say that you and I must meet with those chosen by God. If you do not believe in God, imagine that the universal Mind, the Systemic Forces or Life as a system summon the appropriate people to enhance the evolution of the universe and the progress of humankind.

Your first step, then, is to be attentive. Open your senses to explore your environment and discover the chosen ones. You might only find them by being active. Hope drives us to action. Therefore, make a plan to find your colleagues sent by Life or by the Creator of Life. It might be something like this:

GOAL: to meet people willing to create a better world.

ACTION: sharing with others our need to create a new society.

ACUITY: our goal will be achieved when a certain number of people are ready to form a creative community.

FLEXIBILITY: If we do not find those people, we will contact other groups with similar social interests.

Today, try to meet at least two people who probably want to create a world of justice, peace, fraternity, love, freedom, creativity and so on.

Establish your criteria for the specific *values* those people should have: openness, compassion, generosity, love, creativity, and so forth. You will be more efficient if you include the logical levels in your search for companions. You might use one of the grids you have in chapter IV or the one on the next page. On the page after that, you have an example of how to fill in the grid. Of course, you can use it for other purposes. According to R.Dilts, such a grid coordinates the dreamer, realist and critic.[2]

[2] R.B.Dilts, T.Epstein, R.W.Dilts, *Tools for Dreamers.* Cupertino, CA: Meta Publications, 1991, pp. 323-333.

Dream: _____

What criteria does your goal have to satisfy?

Logical Levels

Where	When	What	How	Why	Who
Contexts	**Time**	**Action**	**Equipment**	**Motive**	**Name & Number**

Outcomes

Dream: DISCOVERING PARTNERS

What criteria does your goal have to satisfy?

THEY MAY BE ANY SORT, REGARDLESS OF SEX, AGE, STATUS, ETC.
BUT THEIR VALUES: OPENNESS, GENEROSITY, COMPASSION, LOVE,
CREATIVITY, JOY, OPTIMISM, HOPE.

Logical Levels

Where	When	What	How	Why	Who
Contexts	**Time**	**Action**	**Equipment**	**Motive**	**Name & Number**
CHURCH	TODAY	TALKING	WORDS	PLEASURE OF GIVING	8 - 10
WORK	DURING ONE MONTH	SHARING DREAMS	ARTICLES	NEED OF CREATING	? ? ?
CLUB	ONE HOUR A DAY	MOTIVATING	BOOKS	PLEASING THE CREATOR	
		GIVING EXAMPLE	VIDEOS		

Objectives

TO FORM A GROUP   TO DEVELOP LEADERSHIP   TO SERVE OTHERS
TO GROW & IMPROVE INDIVIDUALLY   TO DO SOMETHING TO CREATE
A BETTER WORLD

3. BUILDING A CREATIVE COMMUNITY

Suppose you already have a group of people intent on creating a world to which people want to belong. What are the next steps?

My answer is, build together a *creative community* or, if you prefer, a *learning creative community*. In fact I believe in the value of always being in a learning process. I think that organisations, groups and families will improve much more if they are *learning communities*. Thus, I am committed to enhancing the learning attitude in all kinds of groups I work with.

In this section I will mention the main elements of a learning organisation. Of course, I acknowledge that Peter Senge deserves all the credit for explaining such elements.[3]

The idea of learning organisations, however, is very close to the systemic perspective that permeates the NLP technology. In fact, I believe that NLP has many tools to enhance a learning organisation.[4]

Well, let us review the main elements that contribute to developing a learning process within a *creative community*.[5]

A- *All Leaders*

The role of leader is shared within a creative community. Each participant has the right to exert her/his leadership skills, experiencing a special need to be creative while in the role of leader.

[3] P.Senge, *The Fifth Discipline,* o.c.

[4] For example, R.B.Dilts with G.Bonissone, *Skills for the Future.* Cupertino, CA: Meta Publications, 1993. R.B.Dilts, *Strategies of Genius* I-II, Capitola, CA: Meta Publications, 1994.

[5] For further details, Cf. P.Kline & R.Saunders, *Ten Steps to a Learning Organization.* Arlington, VA: Great Ocean, 1993. L.J.González, *Jesus the Leader.* Monterrey, Mexico: Font, 1995.

Each group will decide the specific way to rotate that role. Perhaps during a meeting each one is the leader during a 15-minute period. Or each person is leader during one week.

Some tasks of the leader, are:

— To constantly see the group as a whole, yet simultaneously value each individual as a person.
— To keep a resourceful state in the group and in each participant.
— To keep focusing on the dream and the goals of the group.
— To maintain relations of trust, cooperation and harmony within the group.
— To be more flexible, especially in search of further alternatives and possibilities in all aspects of life.
— To follow the time frame.

B- *Creating a Shared Vision*

Now is the time to transform the personal dreams of creating a better world into a *shared vision*. This is a kind of collective dream. It gathers individual creativity and draws a bigger picture.

When the vision is really shared, it becomes attractive and compelling for the whole group and for each individual. A magnet which draws strength and courage into the group.

A way to create a shared vision is *mindmapping*. Through this technique you involve the right and left brains of the participants. Simultaneously, you are encouraging their creativity. Through mindmapping, their inner artists have the opportunity to deploy their creative resources.

C- *Team Learning for Social Creativity*

Learning in the systemic context means expanding the ability to produce the results we really want in life. Because creativity requires ability if we are to produce the results we really want. And learning's crucial if we are to be creative.

On the other hand, upgrading group learning sounds logical even though it is not so common in our groups and institutions. If we live or work together, it would be normal for us to learn from each other and help each other to learn.

Team learning implies at least two things: sharing our resources and dialogue.

Try the following steps to share your resources:

1- Be aware of what is the best and what is the most beautiful aspect of reality here and now. Enjoy both aspects. Then breathe deeply. Next, trigger a resourceful state.

2- Each participant makes a list of his resources and skills. They write them down on a piece of paper. They read the list of personal resources loudly and clearly.

3- They help each other to extend each person's list. You might see talents that he or she does not see. Simultaneously, it may happen that the other's list makes you aware of some other resources that you have.

4- Plan a specific way to share each other's resources to enhance the learning process within your group.

5- Take action, right now if possible.

Dialogue can be enhanced in your creative community, if you follow these steps:

1- Trigger a resourceful state in the participants.

2- See the group as a whole and care for each individual. Maintain the resourceful state of both the group and the individuals.

3- Let people talk freely about their social dreams.

4- Encourage the participants to listen silently and attentively.

5- If someone disagrees with another person, help him to use *2nd position* with respect to the other, so that he tries to understand the other from his own perspective, thoughts and feelings.

6- If the one who disagrees wishes, he might give the other person an opportunity to make himself understood. Therefore, the first one could ask the other:

"I know you have good reason to say that. Could you let me know those reasons?"

7- Show at least one aspect that distinguishes dialogue from argument. In the latter, people stick to their own point of view and defend it. Dialogue, on the contrary, implies:

  a- Temporarily putting aside our personal opinions
  b- Allowing words to flow freely
  c- Being open to a truth which none of the participants possesses up to now, but which will appear as a result of dialogue.

8- Close the session showing that new aspect of truth which has appeared through dialogue and has enriched the learning process both in the group and in each participant.

D- *Systemic Thinking*

The leadership skill of seeing the group as a whole without neglecting the individuals is already an exercise of systemic thinking.

However, a creative learning community requires this new style of thinking in all areas of its development. It is important, for example, to see the world, society, organisations as systems; otherwise, your creative community won't be able to transcend the *cause-effect explanations*. Systemic thinking will provide it with *structural explanations*.

In that case, your creative community will offer an important discovery: the structural cause of a certain *pattern of behaviour*. A behaviour pattern, as you already know, can represent a problem that keeps repeating itself for years or decades. Economic crises have reappeared in many countries from time to time since the beginning of this century.

You have some exercises on systemic thinking in chapter three. Use them to enhance the learning process within your group.

E- *Self-Leadership*

A creative community presupposes personal mastery on the one hand. On the other hand, it promotes that personal mastery. For example, if you play the role of leader with your group, you will deploy your self-mastery skills. You will suspend your assumptions, you will keep silent to listen to others' point of view, you will forgive others' offences, and so on.

If you do not exert self-leadership, it will be very difficult for you to lead others toward a social creativity on a consistent basis.[6]

I offer you one exercise that approaches just one aspect of self-leadership. It is a very simple but also a very transcendent distinction between *empowering* and *disempowering*. What is empowering awakens your inner artist and makes your resources available. Thus, you are able to use your personal power.

To the contrary, you are disempowered when a word, opinion, or attitude discourages you. Perhaps you believe that the other is right saying that you are stupid. Therefore, you feel unable to deploy your resources. You feel no power within yourself. You are disempowered.

1- Take a comfortable body position. Acknowledge what is the best and what is the most beautiful around you. Enjoy them. Breathe deeply several times. Trigger a resourceful state.

[6] P.Senge, *The Fifth Discipline*, o.c., pp. 139-173. C.C.Manz and H.P. Sims, *Super-Leadership*. New York, NY: Berkley Books, 1990, pp. 52-79.

2- Think of the most frequently disempowering words or sentences you say to yourself and to others. See them clearly on your mental screen. Ask your inner critic, the one who utters them, to avoid saying them in spite of his good intention.

3- Think now which empowering words and sentences you could say to yourself and others. Ask your inner artist for help so that you may invent more affirmations and questions that empower people and yourself. Request even the help of your inner critic to utter those empowering sentences many times a day and to many people.

4- Offer the opportunity to express such sentences within your creative community.

5- Help the participants to make a kind of vow—perhaps offering it to God—to pursue only empowering goals and dreams for the rest of their lives. This attitude of always searching for what is empowering reveals the good quality of self-leadership. It means that a specific individual knows how to lead himself towards the positive and, therefore, away from negative.

6- Share the experience of this exercise.

F- *Mental and Emotional Freedom*

Another aspect of personal mastery or self-leadership is freedom. I emphasise mental and emotional freedom because they can be yours even in the worst circumstances. Dr. Victor Frankl kept this interior freedom while suffering the horrible constraints of a Nazi concentration camp.

Mental freedom has two different aspects. The first refers to your ability to change your mental maps or assumptions. The second is related with the experience of being in a creative group. The latter postulates complete freedom of expression. Everyone is free to express what he thinks or believes.

I suggest you use one of the exercises on systemic thinking or on lateral thinking to enhance the interior freedom to think.

146

As for freedom to express what we think, believe or assume, I will offer an exercise in the next section.

For now, keep in mind that a creative community enhances the freedom to think and to express personal thoughts and beliefs.

Emotional freedom refers to the ability to choose the feelings we want to feel. Perhaps you think that this kind of freedom will make you too cerebral, insensitive, rather cold. No. Emotional freedom is not like that. Authentic interior freedom enriches your emotional life. It gives you more choices and possibilities.

The following exercise is more a suggestion than a technique. Hopefully it may help you to improve your emotional freedom.

1- Take a comfortable body position. Breathe deeply several times. Be aware of what is good and beautiful around you. Choose the best and the most beautiful. Derive pleasure from them. After that, use your anchor to trigger a resourceful state.

2- Call to mind the last time you reacted emotionally to a difficulty, a curse, a painful situation. That is what I would call *zero emotional freedom*. Gregory Bateson calls it "zero learning." He says, "*zero learning* is characterized by *specificity of response,* which—right or wrong—is not subject to correction."[7]

Be aware that such responses prevent you from learning and from using your personal freedom. You should at least experience the need to change, i.e. the will to learn how to use your emotional freedom.

3- Think of the same experience and consider which response you could choose. Perhaps you could have chosen peace and humour instead of anger. Try this right now. Choose a feeling and try to arouse it within your heart.

This is level 1 of emotional freedom. Bateson explains, "*Learning I* is *change in specificity of response* by correction of errors of choice within a set of alternatives." In this case you

---

[7] G.Bateson, *Steps to an Ecology of Mind.* New York, NY: Ballantine, 1985, pp. 279-308.

recognise that you have a set of alternatives—emotional, practical, mental, spiritual. At the emotional level you have many alternatives: sadness, joy, anxiety, peace, hatred, love, despair, hope, pessimism, optimism, and so forth.

4- This time focus on the set of alternatives. Make changes. Create new sets:

> a- **positive:** joy, peace, love, hope, optimism, trust, and so on,
>
> b- **negative:** sadness, depression, anxiety, hatred, despair, mistrust, and so forth.

At least you now have two sets of alternatives from which you can choose your emotional responses. Your freedom to feel has not diminished. On the contrary, it has increased.

"Learning II is *change in the process of Learning I,* e.g., a corrective change in the set of alternatives from which choice is made, or a change in how the sequence or experience is punctuated."

5- Consider now the possibility of enriching your emotional choices by changing the system of sets of feeling. For example, you may gather several feelings around joy, around love, around peace, and so on. Around love you have: compassion, affection, tenderness, predilection, fondness, respect, benevolence, sympathy, admiration, etc. Certainly, your emotional life will grow richer if your choices are richer. You will be like great painters who employ a great variety of colours and shades.

"Learning III is *change in the process of learning II,* e.g., a corrective change in the system of *sets* of alternatives from which choice is made."

6- Write down the changes you intend to achieve at each level of learning or emotional freedom. Plan a way to widen your choices by changing your sets of alternatives.

7- Share your plan with someone else.

A creative community offers its members the atmosphere and techniques that facilitate personal growth and self-leadership.

Without personal mastery it would be very difficult to have a creative learning community.

4. CREATIVE ATMOSPHERE

A group of people committed to social creativity is expected to start at home. If learning means expanding the ability to produce the results we really want, then we must produce certain changes and improvements at home within our family. At least, within our community.

Besides the resourceful state, there are some other states that promote creativity: congruence, acceptance, understanding, freedom.

The first three, congruence, acceptance and understanding, presuppose freedom. Simultaneously, freedom allows the inner artist, and even the inner critic, as well as the realist, to be creative. At the same time, because we are dealing with creativity, freedom is the most basic condition for expressing our personal and group originality.

I observe that Jesus and great leaders throughout human history were able to give freedom and to keep it within their groups. In the same way, we must do our best, even offer our lives, to protect the right people have to express their creativity.

Congruence implies the freedom to express what we are, feel, and think. But this freedom requires one systemic condition: love and respect for others and for our own group. If what you have to say is disempowering for any reason, you should wait for a better occasion to say it. This is the example of Jesus, "I still have many things to say to you but they would be too much for you to bear now. However, when the Spirit of truth comes he will lead you to the complete truth" (Jn 16:12-13).

Your first exercise for today is to practise this attitude or state of congruence.

1- Use your anchor or any other means to trigger in yourself a resourceful state.

2- Search in your heart for a feeling, or an opinion, or a trait of your personality which you would like to share. Ponder whether your self-revelation will empower another person or your group. If you reckon that it could be disempowering, keep it to yourself. You will have a better opportunity later on. Wait.

3- Look for something else that is essentially part of you or what you think or feel. Something that might empower somebody else. Once you have discovered what is empowering, plan a way to share it with that person or with your group.

This kind of sharing, as you know, is basic in AA groups. They neither correct others nor give any counsel. They just share their experience with real congruence. And it works, because experience is the most universal language on this planet.

4- While you deliver your self-revelation, observe the response you elicit in that person or in your group. Take their responses as a feedback to realise whether you are empowering them. If not, introduce commentaries that may facilitate their empowerment.

5- Always maintain an atmosphere of congruence within yourself and within your group. Congruence is just an aspect of creativity. When you create you express the originality of your being, of your thoughts, of your dreams.

6- Share your experience.

The following exercise has to do with *acceptance*. This word is synonymous with respect, love and care. In a systemic context, *congruence* means the skill to express unconditional respect or love for others.

It assumes a basic distinction between the level of *behaviours* and the level of *identity*. Identity—the person as such—is the object of unconditional love. Whereas a negative behaviour is disowned or even rejected.

150

Of course, it is a real art to make others feel accepted and loved, when we do not agree with their motives, ideas, or behaviour.

1- Remember a time when you unconditionally loved someone. Recall her/his face, as if you were reliving that particular moment in your heart. Listen to their voice. Allow your feelings of love and respect to be fully alive. Intensify them. Anchor this state of acceptance. The anchor can be another circle.

Repeat the same procedure with similar experiences. Make your anchor stronger.

2- Keep your state of acceptance. Recall now a loved person who has disappointed you in some way. Perhaps you feel unwilling to think of her/him... Maintain your state of acceptance as you try to think of that person. Distinguish between the personal identity of that loved one and her/his behaviour. Sort out these two levels.

3- Imagine the wonderful beauty of that person's identity. She or he is a living image of God. Their value is infinite. Their possibilities of change and growth are unlimited. In that sense, this person deserves your acceptance.

4- Consider this person's negative behaviour as her/his shadow. Their shadow really belongs to them, but they are not their shadow. It may be ignored or rejected. It exists only because of the light that God or life sheds over that person.

5- Imagine yourself expressing unconditional love to that person, even though you say you disagree with his/her behaviour. Of course, express your disagreement in an empowering way.

6- If possible, take action. Go and express your feelings to that person. Make her/him feel accepted at the level of identity while you disagree with their behaviour.

7- Share your experience.

Understanding is basic within a systems perspective. It allows you to perceive the person's or group's position, point of view, feelings. It would be almost impossible to see the group as a whole and simultaneously to care about each participant without understanding.

Understanding corresponds to *2nd position*. You leave your personal *1st position* and put yourself in another's. Therefore, you can see through his eyes, feel through his heart. This process enables you to understand the other from his personal perspective.

A creative community requires lots of understanding. This is the golden rule for its integration as a system. Even more, understanding empowers people to be creative, simply because you adopt other people's perspective. Then you perceive the natural connection between their personal originality and their dreams, ideas, goals.

1- Use the anchor for a resourceful state first. As soon as you get that state, trigger the state of acceptance.

2- Let someone else or your group express their most original, beneficial—if impossible—ideas on behalf of our world and society.

3- Take *2nd position* to understand their point of view.

4- Search for their help. Ask questions that may help you to understand their perspective. For example, "Could you give me the reasons you have for producing this idea?"

5- Get their feedback. Tell them you understand their point of view, and check whether you have grasped their ideas. Another way to get their feedback and to verify the accuracy of your second position is the simple repetition of their communication. Something like:

— You say that... Do I get your point?
— Do you mean that...?
— So, you believe that...
— I understand that you think... Is it true?
— After your communication I perceive this and this, am I right?
— And other similar expressions.

6- Share this experience to get further feedback.

Continue using the attitudes of congruence, acceptance and understanding in your daily life. Practise them especially at home and in your professional context. In this way they will become habits, i.e real attitudes.

5. TAKING ACTION CREATIVELY

Today's exercise implies taking action on behalf of people. Do something for the good of our society and for the creation of a new and better world. It does not matter how small or insignificant your action may be.

1- Make a plan by yourself or in a group to specify what kind of action you are going to take. Use the steps of the T.O.T.E. or any other structure for planning:

a- GOAL
b- ACTION
c- ACUITY
d- FLEXIBILITY

2- Go to your world and do what you have planned. Perhaps you have decided to keep smiling, to express acceptance, to have more understanding, to search for more people ready to work for a better world, to help a poor person, to visit a sick person.

3- Observe the response that you elicit in people. Jot down the details.

4- Go to your group or search for a person you can share your experience with. Tell him/her what you have learnt or discovered through the process of taking action.

5- Listen carefully to their feedback. Open your heart and mind to further discoveries through their feedback.

6- Enriched by feedback, plan a new action. Better if it is small. But this time place that action within the big picture of our systemic reality. Remember that within a system each part affects the others and the whole system. Therefore, find out in which way you are probably affecting our world with this new action you have planned.

7- Continue this process to the end of your life, if possible. Keep increasing your awareness of your ability to affect the whole system through your creative action.

6. WOMEN'S CONTRIBUTION

Jesus involved women in his leadership. In spite of male dominance in Jewish culture, Luke reports that Jesus "made his way through towns and villages preaching and proclaiming the good news of the kingdom of God. With him went the Twelve, as well as certain women who had been cured of evil spirits and ailments: Mary surnamed the Magdalene, from whom seven demons had gone out, Joanna the wife of Herod's steward Chuza, Susana, and many others who provided for them out of their own resources" (8:1-3).

Women are associated with the creative energy of life at a very deep level. They offer the necessary conditions for a new human life to be born into this world.

Unquestionably, women will play an important role for a new world to be born. Their qualities are required to have a world wholly oriented towards life, justice, love, peace, health, happiness. Women's resources for creating human life will be decisive for the creation of a world to which people want to belong.

I suppose that your group and any creative community will have the grace of women's presence. If not, search for a way to enrich your community with female resources. Perhaps your community or group has only women. In this case explore your own resources and discover which one should be women's contribution to creating a better world.

In any case, whether you are following this creative journey by yourself or you are forming a creative community, find a space for women's specific resources to be integrated.

You may start with a simple exercise of exploration-discovery.

1- Use your anchor or any other means to trigger a resourceful state.

2- Explore women's hearts and personality. Specify the best and most characteristic resources in women:

— Gift of generation
— Altruism
— Compassion
— Suffering
— Spiritual sensitivity
—
—
—

3- Use mindmapping or any other brainstorming technique to discover women's best resources.

4- Classify and select the most important female resources.

5- Dream possibilities and means to enhance those feminine talents that are essential for creating a new world.

6- Plan some ways to test those feminine resources in your family, group, community, school, company, town, and so forth.

7- Take action and transform your dreams and plans into a living process.

8- Share your results with many people, as many as possible. Use the communication media. Open a space for women's resources.

I know from my own experience that it is difficult to recognise, accept and integrate women in our present society. Nevertheless, it is worthwhile to have a social feminine womb for the incubation of a new world. If we want to be systemic, we need women's contribution.

7. A NET OF CREATIVE COMMUNITIES

I hope in the Lord, who has given us the necessary resources to succeed in creating a world to which people want to belong.

If you start a creative community, people will follow you. They need a better world than the present. Even in the rich countries people suffer because of violence, drugs, family disintegration, solitude, illnesses, spiritual insatisfaction, and so forth.

Perhaps some of them will say that they are happy, that they do not need any social change. But if you help them to explore their own lives, they will discover the many possibilities they have to improve. They will realise the need of creating a better world.

When people listen to you talking about your own creative community, at least some of them will feel a deep interest in knowing more about it. Little by little your creative community will be involved in the formation and development of other creative communities.

But even though you are just one community, you will experience the drive to be connected with other groups, movements and institutions that are working for the creation of a new world. For example, think of Dr.M.Scott Peck who has been encouraging all kinds of communities to improve in integration and development. He introduced a method which he called "community building."[8] And more recently he has started "The Foundation for Community Encouragement." The foundation describes its "mission statement" as follows: "The Foundation for

[8] M.Scott Peck, *The Different Drum*. New York, NY: Simon & Schuster, 1988.

Community Encouragement (FCE) encourages people, in a fragmented world, to discover new ways to be together. Living, learning and teaching community principles, we serve as a catalyst for individuals, groups and organisations to:

- communicate with authenticity,
- deal with difficult issues,
- bridge differences with integrity,
- relate with love and respect.

FCE's approach encourages tolerance of ambiguity, the experience of discovery and the tension between holding on and letting go.

As we empower others, so are we empowered by a Spirit within and beyond ourselves."[9]

After reading the FCE mission statement, you may realise that they are doing what I am suggesting in this chapter or during the sixth week of a creative journey. However, it is better for each person or group to start on their own. Later on, they will learn from others.

In fact, the first exercise for today consists of getting in contact with a group, organisation or movement devoted to community building. For example, you could write or phone to the FCE. Jean Vanier's groups are also committed to community building.[10]

The second exercise is better done in a group or at least with somebody else if possible.

---

[9] M.Scott Peck, *A World Waiting to Be Born*. New York, NY: Bantam, 19-93, p. 278.

[10] The address of the FCE is:

The Foundation for Community Encouragement
P.O. Box 449
Ridgefield, Connecticut 06877
U S A
Phone: 203/431-9484
Fax: 203/431-9349

1- Take a comfortable body position. Discover the best and the most beautiful reality in your context. Trigger a resourceful state.

2- Visualise and/or describe possible ways for community building among different movements and parties within your own Church or religion. The goal would be to create a real community of children of God.

3- Visualise and/or describe specific ways to all the different believers, leaders and religions of this planet.

4- Visualise and/or describe possible ways to integrate in one community all the different groups, universities, multinational companies, international clubs, nations, continents, UNO, and all different religions. Just one international family of children of God.

5- Check with your partner or group if you could take any specific action to transform such a great dream into a reality.

VII- SPIRITUAL CREATIVITY

You must be surprised that I have included this chapter on spiritual creativity. You are right. It is something unusual. Only in recent years can we find studies on the spiritual dimension of creativity.[1]

I have several reasons to close this week's creative journey with spiritual creativity. First, I believe that God, the Creator, is the source of our creativity. He decided to share with us His creative power. Therefore, if you work together with Him, He will perfect your personal creativity.

Second, certain dreams like those I suggested in the last chapter, cannot be transformed into reality except by God's power. However, I also believe that God needs our human creativity, our faith and hope to push human history toward that new earth He is going to create.

Third, we human beings require a spiritual experience. According to J.Z.Young, a spiritual experience unifies your nervous system, i.e. all the programs of your brain. And as a result, more endorphines are produced. You get feelings of well-being, serenity and bliss. Therefore, the same author concludes, we need such experiences from time to time. We may have it in the silent contemplation of a beautiful landscape or during a heartfelt religious service.[2]

That spiritual experience corresponds in many cases to the one which Abraham Maslow calls "peak experience." In it are "feelings of limitless horizons opening up to the vision, the feeling

---

[1] J.Cameron with M.Bryan, *The Artist's Way*. New York, NY: G.P.Putnam's Sons, 1992. A.Diaz, *Freeing the Creative Spirit*. New York, NY: HarperSanFrancisco, 1992. D.Goleman, P.Kaufman, M.Ray, *The Creative Spirit*. New York, NY: Dutton, 1992.

[2] J.Z.Young, *Programs of the Brain*. Oxford: Oxford University Press, 1978.

of being simultaneously more powerful and also more helpless than one ever was before, the feeling of great ecstasy and wonder and awe, the loss of placing in time and space with, finally, the conviction that something extremely important and valuable has happened, so that the subject is to some extent transformed and strengthened even in his daily life by such experiences."[3]

For these reasons, I suggest you continue your creative journey at the *spiritual level.*

1. EXPERIENCE OF THE CREATOR'S LOVE

A spiritual experience is valuable for your inner artist because it opens the horizon of limitless creativity. In union with the Creator you can believe more deeply the words of Jesus: "Everything is possible for one who has faith" (Mk 9:24).

If you drink from the eternal Source of Creativity, you will experience a powerful creative energy within yourself. Look at the great leaders throughout human history. Note their humbleness on the one hand, while on the other they were unstoppable in their creativity. They experienced the divine force that drove them to the creation of a better world, of better human relations and, sometimes, of a better connection with our Creator.

You might well ask, "What path should I take to have a deep connection with the eternal Creator, so that I can experience His love and the gracious gift of the creative energy?"

The real answer to this question, according to my experience and knowledge, requires a spiritual life-style. One has an axis: *faith, hope* and *love.* The top end of this axis connects our lives to our Creator, especially through meditation and prayer.

---

[3] A.H.Maslow, *Motivation and Personality.* New York, NY: Harper & Row, 1970, p. 164.

The bottom end of the same axis connects our daily lives with people and nature, especially through love.[4]

Today's exercise might be a further step on your spiritual path, according to your own religious or philosophical beliefs. I invite you to intensify your faith, hope and love. Here is the first part of your assignment.

1- Explore and discover the best and the most beautiful aspects of your reality here and now. Feel them as expressions of our Creator's love. Be grateful to Him.

2- Remember that faith, hope and love have God as their object and centre. Faith makes you believe that He exists and believe what He reveals about Himself, people and nature. So, invent a specific way to practise today, and in the future, this attitude of faith.

3- Hope makes you trust in God without limits. Since He promises lots of blessings, the best of the best and even eternal life, you should foresee a magnificent future for yourself and other people. Visualise health, justice, peace, joy, love, harmony, beauty and happiness. As hope makes you feel certain of having those blessings sooner or later, you can be both optimistic and happy. You get to enjoy those wonderful gifts in advance.

Well, find a way to start hoping now, today, and in the future.

4- Love enables you to create the loved one as a person. Love empowers you to create good things, services, counsels, empowering questions and affirmations for the good of people and nature. When you do good things, God feels loved by you. But, of course, you may use words to express to Him your feelings of devotion, adoration, praise, gratitude, love.

Discover now a specific way to love people, nature, God and yourself. How can you love them and yourself right now, today, and in the future?

[4] I have a longer explanation of these attitudes in L.J.González, *Jesus the Leader*. Monterrey, Mexico: Font, 1995. L.J.González, *Liberación para el amor*. Monterrey, Mexico: Font, 1990.

5- Take action here and now, if possible. Live your faith, hope and love.

6- Share your experience.

If you are a businessman you might think, "What do these three attitudes have to do with work, production, selling, advertising, etc.?"

If you are a businessman, a politician, a scientist, an artist, a teacher, a mother, and so on, just imagine yourself as the Creator's ambassador. He has sent you to this world. He wants you to improve His creation. He wants you to use your creative talents and your specific job to create a better world.

Use faith, hope and love to experience you inner artist as a messenger of good news, a messenger of the Creator, a messenger who preaches the good news of a new world through creative deeds and ideas.

In this way, you are giving a deeper and higher meaning to your daily work and activities. You are not alone. The Creator is always with you. He nourishes your creative energy always and everywhere.

2. ALIGNMENT OF YOUR CREATIVITY

Today you will have the opportunity to review your own life from the perspective of creativity. Imagine your time line as a very wide screen you can watch before you. Something like the following diagram:

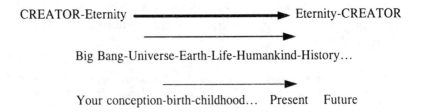

CREATOR-Eternity ⟶ Eternity-CREATOR

⟶

Big Bang-Universe-Earth-Life-Humankind-History...

⟶

Your conception-birth-childhood... Present   Future

You have behind you the Creator and eternity. In the beginning of time and space, the Big Bang started the universe. Then came the cosmic evolution which gave birth to our planet Earth more than four billion years ago. Then life, humankind, history, the history of your own country, the history of your ancestors and, especially, of your parents. Finally, the first moment of your conception is a miracle of creativity. The Creator provided your parents with the ability to create male cells (spermatozoa) and female cells (ova).

At the beginning you were just a masculine cell. When your father put you into your mother's womb, you were creative enough to win the wonderful race of life. You arrived first at the finishing line. You beat out 80 or 90 million competitors who wanted to save their lives by conquering the pearl of life which was your mother's ovum.

So, you exist because you are winner. In general, this is the only way to be a human being. You were creative enough, as a male cell, to win the race of life.

1- Now take a comfortable body posture. Breathe deeply several times. Trigger a resourceful state.

2- Remember a beautiful landscape where you experienced serenity, deep joy, trust and optimism. See again the beauty of that place. Listen to the natural sounds of that spot. Feel in your body the feelings of peace, joy, optimism.

3- Visualise before you the enormous screen representing the Big Bang, the universe, the Earth, human history, your ancestors, your parents, your conception as fruit of your parent's contribution and of your own creative skills. Visualise your birth, your childhood, the next stages of your personal development...

4- Recognise beyond that marvelous screen the eternal now where God lives. See the invisible God with the eyes of your heart which are faith and love. Observe God's love and trust as He gives different talents and resources to each human creature. Highlight His infinite love and predilection for you at the moment when He endows you with precious talents and great resources to be creative like Him. It is His pleasure and glory that you become creative in His image through the use and development of your creative talents.

5- What are your best creative talents? Do you use all of them? Have you used them for people's good, for your own good? Have you developed and multiplied them? Are you like the man entrusted with five talents in Jesus' parable? "The man who had received the five talents came forward bringing five more. 'Sir,' he said, 'you entrusted me with five talents; here are five more that I have made'" (Mt 25:20). Have you doubled your personal talents?

6- After you have reviewed your personal history and the use you have made of your talents, see God's face of light. Enjoy His loving eyes. Listen to His voice within your heart. Feel in your soul (identity) the tenderness of His love. Take your time to experience His infinite love for you.

7- After some minutes, listen more carefully to His words of life. He lives in eternity. Therefore, even though He knows your past, He opens before your eyes the perspective of hope like a wide horizon where numerous possibilities spring up like burgeoning green sprouts. He invites you to gaze at the future with hope. He wants you to transform your horizon into an oasis where your talents grow and give lots of fruit.

8- Answer to the Lord. If you are not a believer, answer to life which also invites you to make the most of your talents and possibilities. Beware of your inner critic. God and life are much more powerful than your inner critic. Shut him up for a while. Let your inner artist express himself. Accept him. Be him. Be a creator created in the Creator's image and likeness. Be the creator you really are.

9- Talk to God, the Creator. Tell Him your present decision. Explain to Him how determined you are. Ask Him to introduce you into the treasure of your talents and resources. Ask Him to give you His own Spirit who is God's creative energy and power.

10- Pace your own future. Imagine yourself in the future as if you were walking on the paths of the world hand-in-hand with the Creator. See yourself at home, in your office, driving through your town, visiting your friends, helping poor people, encouraging human relations and community building. See yourself being a real artist and living an artistic life-style.

11- Find a moment when you can renew your present commitment to the Creator. Every day you need a specific moment to renew your decision to be a creator, a real artist. Perhaps the first moment after you wake up.

12- Share this experience with someone who loves you or with a group of people who respect you and deserve your trust.

Together with that person who loves you, watch again the big screen of creation. Show her/him your creative path within the flow of creative energy God sent when he produced the Big Bang. Show her/him how your own creativity enlarges the river of creative energy which is the universe and especially life. Show her/him how your creative deeds and ideas endure forever in that perfect now of eternity. Enjoy yourselves.

3. THE SCRIPTURES

Besides life interwoven with your personal history, there is another way to feel the presence of the Creator: His own Self-revelation. He reveals Himself in different ways: through creation which is a work of His hands, through the history of Israel, the prophets of the main spiritual traditions.

According to my own faith, the Scriptures for me are the Bible. The Old Testament was revealed to the people of Israel and the New Testament to the followers of Christ.

I will speak of the Bible under one postulate: that you will use the sources of God's revelation according to your own beliefs.

Your first task today and each day is to start reading a page of the Bible. Search for those passages that highlight the talents you have to be creative. Perhaps the first chapters of the book of Genesis, or those passages about Moses' life, or the prophets' life, etc. If you are a Christian read the parable of the talents, the metaphors used by Jesus to describe human identity, "you are the light of the world," etc.

Another possibility, even though you are not a Christian, is the reading of the gospel in order to study Jesus' creativity. He was so creative, that he divided human history in BC—before Christ—and AD—after dominum (the Lord). Learn from Jesus to be creative in your thinking, your language, your metaphors and your way of living.

By yourself, or with your creative community, or with someone else, invent different ways to read the Scriptures. Discover the best way to experience God's empowerment through His own Word. Keep in mind certain sentences of the Scriptures like, "There is nothing I cannot do in the One who strengthens me" (Ph:13).

Your final task for today and for the rest of your life could be the imitation of Jesus' creativity. Although he is the Son of God, he became a real man. Therefore, he used human resources in order to be creative. According to the gospels he made use of his feelings, imagination and lateral thinking.

1- Have a comfortable body posture. Breathe deeply. Be conscious of what is the best and what is the most beautiful around you. Take delight in them.

2- Read from Matthew's gospel two passages of the Sermon on the Mount (5:1-16,38-48).

3- Sense, through faith and intuition, the feelings of Jesus while he was giving that sermon. Try to experience the same feelings at this moment. Help yourself by calling to mind a specific time when you had one of those feelings.

4- Once you are experiencing one of Jesus' probable feelings, read the same texts again. This time search for the images Jesus was visualising while preaching this program-like sermon.

166

Then, do your best to visualise the same images, especially those which are related with a better future for people.

5- Observe now that Jesus employs lateral thinking when he looks at certain traditions from a quite different perspective. Guess the possible questions Jesus asked himself to discover other alternatives for human behaviour. Perhaps he simply kept asking himself again and again, "What else could be a better alternative?"

6- Read once more the same texts. Choose from them a specific behaviour which you are willing to learn or to improve in your daily life. Use lateral thinking to find different alternatives to practise. Choose one of them.

7- If you remember a passage where Jesus exhibits that particular behaviour, read it again. Sense Jesus' feelings, imagery, and thinking.

8- Use Jesus' example to enrich the alternative you have chosen as the best method to practise that behaviour in your daily life.

9- Make a plan of action so that you can start practising that behaviour today:

> GOAL
> ACTION
> ACUITY
> FLEXIBILITY

10- Share your experience of learning from Jesus how to be more creative.

4. PRAYER AND MEDITATION

Jesus recommends a very creative way of praying. It is a way which involves imagination and visualisation, as well as faith and hope: "Everything you ask and pray for, believe that you have it already, and it will be yours" (Mk 11:24).

In this text Jesus recommends, once again, asking. He has already said, "ask, and it will be given to you; search, and you will find; knock, and the door will be open to you. For everyone who asks receives; everyone who searches finds; everyone who knocks will have the door open" (Lk 11:9-10).

So, the first exercise today is prayer. Ask the Creator for more creativity. Ask what you have never asked from him. Invent the best and most wonderful petitions. Do not forget to use your imagination. Visualise yourself as already having whatever you ask for. "Believe that you have it already, and it will be yours," says Jesus.

On the other hand, Jesus follows the classical four steps that characterise silent or contemplative prayer. These four steps are present in prayer practices in the main spiritual traditions like Hinduism, Buddhism, Judaism, Christianism, and Islamism.

Silent prayer is called *meditation* in the scientific field of our days. Dr. Herbert Benson calls it "the relaxation response." He prefers a scientific name in order to skip prejudices and religious discussions.[5]

Jesus' silent prayer or "meditation," as I said before, has the four steps we are supposed to follow according to our own religious faith:

1- A lonely place (Mk 1:35; Lk 5:16; Cf. Mt 6:5-6).
2- An appropriate body posture (Mt 26:39; Mk 14:35; Lk 22:41).
3- A loving attention to God (following Jesus' example, we may repeat: "Father, I love you." Mt 6:9, Lk 3:21-22).
4- Placing thoughts aside (Mt 6:7).

Conclusion: to foresee a better future in hope (Mk 11:24).

[5] H.Benson with M.Z.Klipper, *The Relaxation Response*. New York, NY: Avon, 1976.

During meditation your whole nervous system is unified. Your brain behaves as a unity. Your emotional state becomes resourceful and appropriate for creativity.[6] Thus, I highly recommend the daily practice of meditation. Twenty minutes in the morning and twenty minutes in the evening is the time meditation requires to produce its beneficial effects in your body, mind, feelings, and relations either with God or with other people.

To effectively practise meditation, breathe deeply at the beginning, if you wish. Change your state. Surely the state of love is the most appropriate for meditation.

1- Go to a lonely place.

2- Take a comfortable body posture, but keep your spinal cord straight.

3- Focus your mind on loving the Creator according to your belief system. Repeat again and again a short sentence of love: "God, I love you." "God, I love you." "God, I love you."

4- As soon as you notice that you are thinking of something else, put your thoughts aside. Do not struggle to avoid those thoughts. Just leave them and come back to the Lord, our loving Creator.

5- Conclusion. Concentrate on hope just now. Foresee yourself changed, improved, having creative solutions, ideas and inventions. Say to your Creator: "Lord, I see myself different, creative, living an artistic life, because I hope in You. And having hope, I'll do my best to be the creative artist who was created in Your image and likeness."

Dr. Benson recommends to express to the Lord our need of creativity at the very beginning of our meditation. Afterwards, during meditation, we just let it go. We focus our mind and heart on Him, our Creator. By doing so, we offer our unconscious

---

[6] H.Benson with W.Proctor, *Your Maximum Mind*. New York, NY: Avon, 1989, pp. 175-180.

mind, our inner artist, and even God, the opportunity to incubate the idea or solution we are searching for.

When we adopt this attitude of surrender, as if we were repeating to our Father and Creator, "thy will be done on earth as it is in heaven," that is what orientals call *no-mind*. This is a state of complete absorption in what one is doing. Professor K. Kraft, a Buddhist scholar at Lehigh University who spent many years in Japan, says, "In Zen they use the word *mind* in a very interesting way. The word is also a symbol for the consciousness of the universe itself. In fact, the mind of the individual and the mind of the universe are regarded as ultimately one. So by emptying oneself of one's smaller, individual mind, and by losing the individual's intense self-consciousness, we are able to tap into this larger, more creative, universal mind."[7]

Your task for the following weeks includes several aspects. Try different ways of silent prayer or meditation. But, according to Dr. Benson's research, you are better off meditating within the flow of your own religious beliefs.

After you have explored different meditation methods, discover the one which fits your personality, your own history, and your specific way of relating with our Creator.

Later on, invent a method of meditation that includes the above four or five steps, your religious background, your historic and social circumstances. Invent a new method of prayer.

5. LOVE: CREATING BETTER PEOPLE

At the human level the best and most concrete expression of the human spirit is love. Through love we transcend ourselves. Love frees us from the chains that keep us shut in the prison of our selfishness.

---

[7] Quoted by D.Goleman, P.Kaufman, M.Ray, *The Creative Spirit,* o.c., p. 47.

Most of all, love allows our inner artist to reach the peak of his creativity. Through love our inner artist creates the other. Through love he encourages the loved one to be the person she/he is meant to be.

I have emphasised this great possibility several times. Nevertheless, I insist on the creative power of love, because it belongs to the very core of our spiritual dimension. Great people, saints, prophets, religious leaders have discovered that love is the surest way to be connected with our Creator. Therefore, fraternal love represents one of the best expressions of our spiritual creativity.

Nowadays, especially in the business world, love has a new name: *service*.

In the late '80s business people became extremely aware of the value of service. They had tangible proofs to demonstrate that an intangible like service "pays handsomely."[8] But what is more surprising is the explanation of service. Ron McCann emphasises that service pays when it stems from our hearts. In fact, McCann says that one serves for love not for money.[9]

Certainly, service requires a constant measurement of customer satisfaction. Tom Peters suggests the following items.[10]

1- *Frequency*. Formal surveys claim every 60 to 90 days are a must.

2- *Format*. A questionnaire is a basic instrument. Informal groups of a few customers should be called to every operation—manufacturing, distribution, accounting, not just marketing.

3- *Content*. Ask some standard quantifiable questions.

4- *Design of content*. Listen systematically and "naively" from as many perspectives as possible.

---

[8] T.Peters, *Thriving on Chaos*. New York, NY: Harper & Row, 1988, pp. 108-129.

[9] R.McCann, *The Joy of Service*. Service Information Source Publications.

[10] T.Peters, *Thriving on Chaos*, o.c., pp. 124-125.

5- *Involve everyone.* Besides customers, include all kinds of people in your company or group, of all functions and all levels of seniority.

6- *Measure everyone's satisfaction.* Measure the satisfaction of all direct and indirect customers, and every member of the distribution channel—dealer, retailer, wholesaler, franchisee, rep, etc.

7- *Combination of measures.* Reduce measures to a composite quantitative score for some individuals (salespersons, service persons) groups (centre team), facilities, divisions.

8- *Relation to compensation and other rewards.* Include your people in compensation plans (incentives, gain-sharing, etc.).

9- *Symbolic use of measures.* Key customer satisfaction measures should be publicly posted in every part of the organisation.

Having this example, use your creativity both to evaluate your service to other people and improve its quality. You might discover new ways to train people in service, to perfect service in groups, companies, religious institutions, and so forth.

1- Take a comfortable body posture. Breathe deeply. Think of the best and the most beautiful things in your existence. Derive pleasure from these two things.

2- Watch your time line within the big screen that you have already imagined. See your own life. Observe your service and ask yourself the following questions:

— Do I serve others out of love?
— Does my love mean the will to help them satisfy their healthy needs?
— Does my love mean an authentic search for the personal improvement of others?
— Does my love contribute to the creation of other people in the sense of facilitating their process of becoming persons?

— Am I aware of the joy and pleasure that stem from service?
— Do I contribute to people's satisfaction even when I have to give a negative answer?
— Am I ready to say *no* when people demand a service which does not benefit them?

3- Make an effective questionnaire to measure the level of satisfaction that your service produces in others.

4- Make a plan to apply that questionnaire or any other instrument to measure the degree of satisfaction your service causes in people around you.

5- Clarify which people, which activities and which circumstances require a better service from you.

6- Find out the resources you have to improve the quality of your service, especially in the above cases.

7- Make a specific plan to deploy your resources for the improvement of your service.

8- Give to your future improved service a spiritual dimension: do it out of love for people and for God who is at our service from all eternity.

9- Share your discoveries, plans and spiritual perspective with someone else or with your group.

6. THE SPIRITUAL AND CREATIVE VALUE OF SUFFERING

Dr. Victor Frankl, after having spent four years in a Nazi concentration camp, discovered the spiritual value of suffering. Our pain and sorrow offer an opportunity to search for the real meaning of life. Suffering makes us find a trove of values that, like stars, show us where the north is.

Besides that, still from Dr. Frankl's perspective, suffering frees us. The reason is that it gives us the chance to use our interior freedom. Whether we like it or not, suffering makes us choose an attitude. We might decide to be angry and rebellious, or peaceful and patient. Our choice can be empowering or disempowering, but it will stem from our freedom, never as a direct effect of suffering.

From this perspective, suffering appears like an instrument of life or, better, an expression of our Creator's love. Both God and His creature life use pain and suffering to shape the most essential traits and features of identity.

What's more, through Jesus dying for love on the cross, God revealed His power to transform our suffering into a path to resurrection, which is complete freedom from suffering, evil and death. Simultaneously, resurrection is the total possession of life, happiness and perfection.

A.Robbins arrived at a similar conclusion about pain and suffering. He discovered, from the NLP perspective, that pain is able to drive us towards radical change and improvement. He explains, "one of the things that turns virtually anything around is reaching a *pain threshold*. This means experiencing pain at such an intense level that you know you *must change now*—a point at which your brain says, 'I've had it; I can't spend another day, not another *moment*, living or feeling this way."[11]

So pain and suffering obviously make us change and improve, if we want to. However, our suffering imposes its power on us when we reach our *pain threshold*. As Robbins says, we think, "I've had it." "No more!" "That's it!"

In this case, when suffering makes us change, it is clear that our pain is used by life or by the Creator as an instrument of his love. He wants us to improve. Therefore, he tolerates our suffering. Perhaps, he wants us to suffer in order to open for us the horizon of resurrection.

[11] A.Robbins, *Awaken the Giant Within.* New York, NY: Simon & Schuster, 1991, p. 130.

Some psychologists, Philipp Lersch for example, consider suffering as a necessary condition to deploy our creativity. He summarises his observations in one sentence of Meister Eckhart, "suffering is the quickest horse to reach perfection."

An artist, an inventor, a creative professional and a person who introduces positive changes in our society has a lot to suffer. He or she suffers rejection, renounces certain pleasures for the sake of research, work, inventions. He or she suffers from lack of money and support. And so on.

So, pain and suffering are part of our creative journey. Hopefully you have understood their value. In this case, your exercise for today is to choose pain deliberately. Choose it not because of suffering, but because of its generative quality. In fact, pain is generative in the sense of generating change, improvement, perfection. Most of all, at least in certain spiritual traditions, pain endured for love intensifies the flow of our spiritual life. As a result, it takes us closer to God and closer to our fellow men and women.

1- Sit down. Take a comfortable body posture. Breathe deeply. Think of the best and the most beautiful things around you. Enjoy them. Acknowledge that they are expressions of God's love for you. Choose and feel a state of love right now.

2- Look at that big screen where you can contemplate the whole span of your life. Be aware of the presence of pain and suffering along the path of your life.

3- Distinguish between real suffering—with an objective cause—and imagined suffering caused just by your interpretations and thoughts.

4- Knowing that God wants you to be joyful and happy, refrain from creating any sort of unnecessary suffering. For example, instead of focusing on negative or disempowering attitudes, behaviours and situations, focus on the empowering ones. In this way you avoid unnecessary suffering.

5- Choose, from your heart, freely and with lots of love, those situations, renouncements, behaviours which are painful, but contribute to your growth, creativity, union with God and suffering people.

Imagine yourself renouncing a food which is not healthy. Visualise yourself taking time to achieve your dreams. See yourself visiting sick people, helping the poor, being faithful to your wife, and so on.

6- Foresee situations where your inner artist will be confronted with pain and suffering. Ask the Lord for help. Put your hope in Him and visualise yourself using that suffering to grow as a person and become more creative.

7- Share your experience with someone else.

7. YOUR CREATIVE MISSION

The achievement of your mission on earth will impose a lot of suffering on you. It is difficult to be the one you are meant to be. It is like giving birth to yourself every day. Like a woman in labour you will pant with pain. But insofar as you are born and grow, your creativity to achieve your mission will improve.

From the NLP perspective, your mission—as a person or as a group—stems from your identity. The uniqueness of your personal being determines your mission. I mean, your more specific mission.

If you are a doctor, your mission is to improve health and complete well-being. If you are a mother, your mission is to be a great mother. If you are an artist, your mission is to increase the beauty of the universe.

Beyond your most evident mission there is at least another one: to be an artist trained by the Creator. At this level I agree with Julia Cameron who says, "the heart of creativity is an experience of the mystical union; the heart of the mystical union is an experience of creativity. Those who speak in spiritual terms routinely refer to God as the creator but seldom see *creator* as the literal term for *artist*. I am suggesting you take the term *creator* quite literally. You are seeking to forge a creative alliance, artist-to-artist with the Great Creator. Accepting this concept can greatly expand your creative possibilities."[12]

The mystical union with God, however, is not so easy. It demands a total perfection in love and a complete freedom from any sin, from any voluntary imperfection. Most of all, it depends on God's grace. It is God's gift. You cannot get such union relying only on your effort and capabilities. Nevertheless, God only grants this gift to those who want it and work for it.

But, when the person's effort and God's grace come together, "a creative alliance, artist-to-artist" takes place. My favourite example is St. John of the Cross, the famous Spanish mystic who was born in 1542 near to Avila, in Spain. Inspired by St.Teresa of Avila, he reformed the Carmelite Order and founded the Discalced Carmelite Order.

Viewed as rebellious and disobedient, he was put into prison in the Carmelite monastery of Toledo. The cell was so small that he could not stand. In utter darkness, and an erstwhile toilet, it stank. He was fed just bread, sardines and water. Three days a week only bread and water. These three days he was taken out of that horrible tomb for his ration of lashings. The wounds caused by those lashes took years to heal properly.

In spite of so much pain and suffering, John of the Cross managed to write the best poems in Spanish literature and, simultaneously, the best religious poems in the universe. How is it possible?

At that time he was living the mystical union with God. He loved God with all his heart, with all his soul, with all his strength and with all his mind. Thus he was able to focus on his experience of God's love, on God's beauty and on the beauty of this world. For example, he described such experience in a very creative way. Let us read some stanzas of the poem he wrote in his prison. The subject of the poem says to the Lord:

[12] J.Cameron with M.Bryan, *The Artist's Way,* o.c., p. 2.

Reveal Your presence,
And may the vision of Your beauty be my death;
For the sickness of love
Is not cured
Except by Your very presence and image.

Later on, when the person has experienced the presence of the Lord, he describes his experience with the following beautiful imagery:

My Beloved is the mountains,
And lonely wooded valleys,
Strange islands,
And resounding rivers,
The whistling of love-stirring breezes,

The tranquil night
At the time of the rising dawn,
Silent music,
Sounding solitude,
The supper that refreshes, and deepens love.

Here we have a good example of the creative fruits produced by the mystical union with God.

Not all people can be poets, painters, inventors, scientists, geniuses. That is true. However, we all are called to the mystical union with God. You could argue that only very few people have reached such a high level of spiritual development. Very few derive their artistic inspiration from a direct union with the Great Creator. You are right. But the fact that few people achieve a Ph.D. in their studies does not mean that the others are incompetent.

God is generous without limits. So much, that He wants to share not only His creativity, but also His love, wisdom, beauty, and goodness with each of us. If we do not attain that mystical union here on earth, God will achieve His purpose in heaven. You won't escape from His love. He will share with you the best of

His divinity for all eternity. Then your creativity will be God's creativity.

Your task for today and for each day is to try to express something with all your will, with all your faith, with all your hope and with all your love. Say it as soon as you get up and as many times as possible during the day:

— Lord, I want your gift to be an artist in mystical union with You, the eternal Artist.

CONCLUSION

After I have tried my best to stir your intuition so that you may glimpse the greatness of your being, your enormous resources, and the possibilities of your inner artist, I realise how far I am from accurately describing the dazzling beauty of your personal identity.

However, I trust in the Great Creator. He will introduce you into the path of self-discovery and self-expression through the experience of an increasing creativity.

In fact, the Creator needs your creativity to continue the improvement of His creation. He wants you to be a creator in the original sense of this word. Of course, He wants you to be a creator like Him, i.e. a creator of possibilities, of goodness, of beauty, of people, of a better and more human world.

Our loving Creator wants you to be a creator not only for the benefit of others, but also for your own happiness and fulfilment. If you do not improve in creativity every day, you risk failing as a human being. You will be like an apple tree which does not give any fruit. Therefore, you won't be the person you are meant to be. Even worse, you won't be happy.

Life is a creative energy. Observe the plants, animals, human beings. Verify that life is creative by its very nature. Life cannot not be creative. Since you are alive, you have the same creative energy that characterises life. Furthermore, because of your human talents, you can surpass the limits of life's creativity.

In fact, you can exceed nature's creativity because of your thinking skills. Through these you may adopt different perspectives, find out more alternatives, look at the wholeness of the big picture, discover new possibilities, invent tools, devices and products. You can also create intangibles like service, solutions and learning methods.

That's a fact. The Great Creator decided to improve His creation through your personal creativity. The Lord is all-powerful. However, He shares His power with you and with each human being. He endowed us with lots of talents in order to share with us the pleasure and joy of creating.

Yes. I agree with those psychologists who have discovered that creativity is a source of pleasure and happiness. You may feel the need to create not only out of compassion and love, but also out of your own creative being and the need of joy and happiness.

In brief, you can look at your own being from different perspectives. And each of them will highlight the features of an artist in your personal identity. You are an artist or a creator, as you prefer. God created you as a creative artist. Life endowed you with its creative energy. People require your creativity to improve in freedom, justice, fraternity, love, happiness. Our world demands your creative investment, i.e. instead of using your talents to destroy nature, use them to preserve its natural balance and harmony. Finally, your own human nature—endowed with thinking skills, intuition, an unconscious mind and many other resources—requires your personal creativity so that you may reach the fullness of your identity: an artist created in the image of the eternal Artist, and adopted by Him as His child.

The answer to all these requests and demands is your own responsibility. You have the ability to respond for your creative talents and your creative identity: you *are* creator and artist.

BIBLIOGRAPHY

Anderson, H.H. (Ed.) *Creativity and its Cultivation*. New York, NY: Harper & Row, 1959.

Bateson, G., *Steps to an Ecology of Mind*. New York, NY: Ballantine, 1985.

Bateson, G., *Mind and Nature: A Necessary Unity*. New York, NY: Bantam, 1988.

Benson, H. with Klipper, Z., *The Relaxation Response*. New York, NY: 1976.

Benson, H. with Proctor, W., *Beyond the Relaxation Response*. New York, NY: Times Books, 1984.

Benson, H. with Proctor, W., *Your Maximum Mind*. New York, NY: Avon, 1989.

Blakeslee, T.R., *The Right Brain*. New York, NY: PBJ Books, 1983.

Brockman, J. (Ed.) *Creativity*. New York, NY: Simon & Schuster, 1993.

Buzan, T., *Make the Most of Your Mind*. New York, NY: Simon & Schuster, 1988.

Buzan, T., *Use Both Sides of Your Brain*. New York, NY: Penguin, 1991.

Cameron, J. with Bryan, M., *The Artist's Way*. New York, NY: G.P. Putnam's Sons, 1992.

Chalvin, D., *Utiliser tout son cerveau*. Paris: ESF Editeur, 1989.

Chalvin, D., Rubaud, C., *Utilisez toutes les capacités de votre cerveau*. Paris: ESF Editeur, 1990.

De Bono, E., *Lateral Thinking*. New York, NY: Harper & Row, 1993.

De Bono, E., *De Bono's Thinking Course*. New York, NY: Facts On File, 1994.

De Brabandere, L., Mikolajczak, A., *Le plaisir des idées*. Paris: Dunod, 1994.

Diaz, A., *Freeing the Creative Spirit*. New York, NY: HarperSanFrancisco, 1992.

Dilts, R., Grinder, J., Bandler, R., DeLozier, J., *Neuro-Linguistic Programming* II, Cupertino, CA: Meta Publications, 1980.

Dilts, R.B., Epstein, T., Dilts, R.W., *Tools for Dreamers*. Cupertino, CA: Meta Publications, 1991.

Dilts, R.B. with Bonissone, G., *Skills for the Future*. Cupertino, CA: Meta Publications, 1993.

Dilts, R.B., *Strategies of Genius* I-II, Capitola, CA: Meta Publications, 1994.

Frankl, V.E., *Man's Search for Meaning*. New York, NY: Pocket, 1985.

Fritz, R., *The Path of Less Resistance*. New York, NY: Columbine, 1989.

Fritz, R., *Creating*. New York, NY: Fawcett Columbine, 1991.

Gamache, R.D. and Kuhn, R.L., *The Creativity Infusion*. New York, NY: HarperCollins, 1989.

Gawain, S., *Creative Visualization*. New York, NY: Bantam, 1982.

Gawain, S., *Living in the Light*. New York, NY: Bantam, 1993.

Goleman, D., Kaufman, P., Ray, M., *The Creative Spirit*. New York, NY: Dutton, 1992.

González, L.J., *Liberación para el amor*. Monterrey, Mexico: Font, 1990.

González, L.J., *Psychology of Personal Excellence*. Monterrey, Mexico: Font, 1993.

González, L.J., *Jesus the Leader*. Monterrey, Mexico: Font, 1995.

González, L.J., *Pleasure in Problem-Solving*. Monterrey, Mexico, 1995.

Kline, P. & Saunders, B., *Ten Steps to a Learning Organization*. Arlington, VA: Great Ocean, 1993.

Koestler, A., *The Act of Creation*. New York, NY: Penguin, 1989.

Maslow, A.H., *Motivation and Personality*. New York, NY: Harper & Row, 1970.

Manz, C.C. and Sims, H.P., *Super-Leadership*. New York, NY: Berkley Books, 1990.

May, R., *The Courage to Create*. London: Collins, 1976.

Ornstein, G.R. and Thompson, R.F., *The Amazing Brain*. Boston, MA: Houghton and Mifflin Co., 1986.

Peters, T., *Thriving on Chaos*. New York, NY: Harper & Row, 1988.

Peters, T., *Liberation Management*. New York, NY: Alfred A.Knopf,

Rainer, T., *The New Diary*. Los Angeles, CA: Jeremy P.Tarcher, 1978.

Ray, M. & Myers, R., *Creativity in Business*. New York, NY: Doubleday, 1989.

Robbins, A., *Awaken the Giant Within*. New York, NY: Simon & Schuster, 1991.

Robles, T., *Concierto para cuatro cerebros*. Mexico: Instituto Milton Erickson, 1990.

Rof Carballo, J., *Medicina y Actividad Creadora*. Madrid: Revista de Occidente, 1964.

Russel, P., *The Brain Book*. New York, NY: Penguin, 1979.

Scott Peck, M., *A Different Drum*. New York, NY: Simon & Schuster, 1988.

Scott Peck, M., *A World Waiting to Be Born*. New York, NY: Bantam, 1993.

Senge, P.M., *The Fifth Discipline*. New York, NY: Doubleday, 1990.

Stone, H. & Stone, S., *Embracing Your Inner Critic*. New York, NY: HarperSanFrancisco, 1993.

Thompson, C.C., *What a Great Idea!* New York, NY: HarperCollins, 1992.

Weisberg, R.W., *Creativity*. New York, NY: W.H. Freeman, 1992.

Wonder, J. & Donovan, P., *Whole-Brain Thinking*. New York, NY: William Morrow, 1984.

Wycoff, J., *Mindmapping*. New York, NY: Berkley Books, 1991.

Yeager, J., *Thinking About Thinking*. Cupertino, CA: Meta Publications, 1985.

Young, J.Z., *Programs of the Brain*. Oxford: Oxford University Press, 1978.